Research and Development in School

Research and Development in School

Grounded in Cultural Historical Activity Theory

By

May Britt Postholm

BRILL
SENSE

LEIDEN | BOSTON

All chapters in this book have undergone peer review.

The Library of Congress Cataloging-in-Publication Data is available online at http://catalog.loc.gov

Typeface for the Latin, Greek, and Cyrillic scripts: "Brill". See and download: brill.com/brill-typeface.

ISBN 978-90-04-41019-0 (paperback)
ISBN 978-90-04-41020-6 (hardback)
ISBN 978-90-04-41021-3 (e-book)

Copyright 2019 by Koninklijke Brill NV, Leiden, The Netherlands.
Koninklijke Brill NV incorporates the imprints Brill, Brill Hes & De Graaf, Brill Nijhoff, Brill Rodopi, Brill Sense, Hotei Publishing, mentis Verlag, Verlag Ferdinand Schöningh and Wilhelm Fink Verlag.
All rights reserved. No part of this publication may be reproduced, translated, stored in a retrieval system, or transmitted in any form or by any means, electronic, mechanical, photocopying, recording or otherwise, without prior written permission from the publisher.
Authorization to photocopy items for internal or personal use is granted by Koninklijke Brill NV provided that the appropriate fees are paid directly to The Copyright Clearance Center, 222 Rosewood Drive, Suite 910, Danvers, MA 01923, USA. Fees are subject to change.

This book is printed on acid-free paper and produced in a sustainable manner.

Contents

Preface   IX
List of Illustrations   X

1   Introduction   1
   1   Development Work Research and Research in School   1
   2   DWR and Research at Valen School   1
   3   The Aim of the Book   5
   4   The Structure of the Book   6

2   Theoretical Perspectives and Cultural Historical Activity Theory   8
   1   Different Theoretical Perspectives   8
   2   Cultural Historical Activity Theory   11
   3   The Activity System: Its Origin and Development   13
   4   Researching Development Processes   19

3   The Qualitative Method: Its Historical and Theoretical Roots and Characteristics   25
   1   Introduction   25
   2   Historical Roots   25
   3   Theoretical Roots   29
   4   Characteristics of the Qualitative Method   33

4   Researcher Roles and Access to the Research Field   41
   1   Introduction   41
   2   Researcher Roles and the Aim of the Research   41
   3   Access to the Research Field   47

5   Qualitative Research Approaches and Analysis   51
   1   Introduction   51
   2   Case Studies   52
   3   Ethnographic Studies   55
   4   Phenomenological Studies   58
   5   Narrative Studies   62
   6   Text Analysis   65
   7   Conversation Analysis   66

6 Data Collection 68
1. Introduction 68
2. Observation as a Data Collection Strategy 68
3. Different Observer Roles 69
4. Interviews as a Data Collection Strategy 71
5. Types of Interviews 72
6. Questions That Help the Researcher Achieve Understanding 73
7. Connection between Interview and Observation 80
8. Practical Advice 81

7 Analysing the Data Material Using the Constant Comparative Analysis Method and D-Analysis 85
1. Introduction 85
2. The Point of Departure and Purpose of the Constant Comparative Analysis Method 86
3. The Importance of Theory When Using the Constant Comparative Analysis Method 87
4. Analytical Procedures in the Constant Comparative Analysis Method 90
5. Analysis of an On-Going Process 98
6. Contextual Circumstances in the Analysis 98
7. Asking Questions and Making Comparisons 99
8. Strategies in the Analytical Work 100
9. Categories and Structure in a Written Presentation 102
10. Background for the Project Used as an Example for the Constant Comparative Analysis Method and D-Analysis 103
11. Concluding Reflection 109

8 Quality and Ethics 110
1. Introduction 110
2. Knowledge – Constructed and Intersubjective 110
3. Concepts Representing Quality 111
4. Ethical Principles in Research 117
5. Quality and Ethics – A Summary 119

9 Writing up the Research Project 121
1. Introduction 121
2. The Thesis and the Researcher's Position 121
3. The Recipients of the Thesis 122
4. The Introduction in the Thesis 123
5. Thick and Thin Descriptions 126

6 How to Structure the Text   126
7 Descriptions as the Starting Point for Further Analysis   130
8 Quotations Embedded in the Text   131
9 The Connecting Theme in the Master's Thesis   133

Appendix 1: Sample Letter of Consent   135
Appendix 2: Interview Guide for Shadowed Teachers   137
Appendix 3: Overview of Data Material Collected in School A1   138
References   140
Index   150

Preface

This book has grown out of my belief that researchers must develop practice while also conducting research on it. Having used cultural historical activity theory (CHAT) as a theoretical framework in several research projects in school, I have found that this theory has both a theoretical foundation and well-developed models that are good tools for collective change processes. In Norway, development and research are commonly combined as evidenced by the term R&D work. In CHAT, as development comes first, the proper term for the concept is development work research (DWR). In my opinion this is the more correct term, as research is carried out on processes that are actively taking place and on development processes that have been implemented. In DWR the researcher collaborates with practitioners, in school this would be teachers and leaders, to develop areas practitioners feel are in need of improvement. Theory, represented by the researcher, and practice can then be combined in DWR, a combination that has been a challenge in change and development processes in school. The researcher could be a person coming to the school, or a teacher or leader in school could guide and conduct DWR. When teachers and leaders are working on a Master's degree and conducting both research and DWR in their own and possibly other schools to collect data and develop knowledge, they can create knowledge-based development processes and useful knowledge can be developed on an on-going basis.

However, little has been written about the methodological approaches that can be applied when CHAT is the framework for research. I examine how research and development may be combined in Chapter 2. The methodology that is chosen will depends on the research questions asked. CHAT provides direction and the framework for collective development, but the motivation lies in the object. This means that the launch of the project is important as everyone must understand what the aim is and thus find the motivation to take part in the initiated processes. My wish is that CHAT and its models will be able to contribute to the development processes we want to see in school, which in turn will promote the pupils' learning outcome.

Illustrations

Figures

2.1 Overview of constructivist theories.   10
2.2 Vygotsky's triangle showing the intermediate stage between stimulus and response via X, an aid.   14
2.3 The activity system.   14
2.4 The expansive learning cycle.   17
2.5 The action learning circle.   19
2.6 The R&D model.   23
3.1 Overview of theories on different levels.   30
3.2 A vase, a serving plate and two faces.   31
3.3 From broad to narrow research question.   38
6.1 Example of observation note.   81
7.1 Overview of main categories, sub-categories and core categories.   95
9.1 Structure of a chapter.   129
9.2 Structure and content in a Master's thesis.   133

Table

7.1 Visualisation of a coding and categorisation process.   92

CHAPTER 1

Introduction

1 Development Work Research and Research in School

Below I will develop some ideas about an imagined project a school principal and a teacher will be leading to improve practices on both the school and classroom level. The teacher's task is to support the leaders in their school development work research (DWR). This refers to a research approach that has been developed in cultural historical activity theory (CHAT). In Chapter 2 I will examine both CHAT and DWR in more detail. When taking a DWR approach, traditional qualitative methodologies can also be used to research the processes. I will call the principal Helene and the teacher Erik. They want to research development processes and conduct traditional qualitative research. The goal when conducting traditional qualitative research is not development *per se*, but they can obtain new knowledge that can be used in future development processes. Master's degree students will also be collecting data at this school for the thesis they will be writing.

2 DWR and Research at Valen School

Erik has worked for six years at Valen school. A comprehensive lower secondary school (Years 1 to 10) in a satellite town close to a large city in Norway, this school has 320 pupils and 38 teachers. Erik is studying for a Master's degree, and in the coming year he will be writing his thesis. His paper will focus on development activities in his school and will be based on research conducted there. His focus will be on DWR, and this is made to order for him as he has been given responsibility for leading development activities in the school together with Helene. Helene, who has been the principal for five years, has just completed a Master's degree in school leadership that has taught her about leading DWR in school. Helene worked as a teacher for eight years in another comprehensive school (Years 1 to 10) before she applied for the principal position. The school where she worked as a teacher was not particularly development oriented so she finds it reassuring to have Erik on the team and leading the development activities in her new school. Erik is known for having an inquisitive and critical approach to his teaching where he is always thinking of ways to improve.

After he graduated, Erik has worked in Valen school at the lower secondary level. He has participated in development activities that have involved the entire school earlier, but he has never led work like this project. Through his participation in development work he has gained some experience which he believes will help him now that he will be at the helm of such a project. Even though he is working at the lower secondary level, he has shared teaching experience with colleagues from all levels in the school so he knows what has been successful and what is more problematic. But he feels he knows the lower secondary level best since this is where he works and the area where he has been collaborating most with his colleagues. He admits to himself that he needs to acquire a deeper understanding of how they approach development work on the primary level so he will be better equipped to lead the work with these teachers.

An earlier DWR project in the school was supported by researchers from the local university. In this work the teachers at the three levels (Years 1–4, 5–7 and 8–10) wanted to start out with different topics and development questions. The primary level (Years 1–4) had been working with "differentiated teaching with focus on assessment", whereas the upper primary level had been working on "differentiated teaching with focus on organization and facilitation", and the lower secondary level teachers wanted to work with "varied ways of working and learning". The development question for the teachers at the lower secondary level was: "How can different ways of working with focus on learning strategies contribute to the social and academic development of each pupil?" This question was developed in collaboration with the teachers and the researcher working on this level. The school leader had decided that the curriculum should be the basis for choosing the topic, and it turned out that this did not restrict the choices the teachers had: there were more than enough interesting topics for them to choose from.

Erik has to find a way to plan the process for choosing a topic for the development work that is to be set in motion in the school. He and Helene have to reflect on whether all the teachers should be working with the same topic, or whether the three levels should choose independently of each other within the current curriculum. If the teachers are working on different topics, they can still come together in plenary sessions to share experiences, Erik thinks, but sharing across levels may not be as productive for everyone, which is the intention and hope, as they are not all involved in the same things. Nevertheless, Erik thinks, what is most important is that they get to work with something they feel needs to be developed. He had read that the content of development activities must come "from below" and "from within", which means that what must be in focus is development the teachers feel is needed. In this context

Erik realises the similarities between the way pupils and teachers learn. He has found that pupils learn most when they are motivated and when they get to work with content they feel is relevant for them. For this reason Erik also appreciates the project work method, which is based on the interests of the pupils in interaction with the curriculum goals. He has also read research that claims teachers learn and develop their teaching practice best if they can work on areas where they feel the need to learn more and develop. Why else would they spend time on development activities, Erik asks himself. Erik and Helene have discussed how they probably need support from external resource persons in the work in the school and are thinking about inviting teacher educators/researchers to contribute knowledge about topics they are working with and to support the development processes.

Helene and Erik are both familiar with methodologies for teachers' learning, such as action learning and lesson study, and have also read about the IGP method (individual, group, plenum) as a model for launching development work. They have been informed about development work at one school working with classroom management as their topic area. In the first semester the IGP model was used where the teachers were instructed to first to think through individually what was important for them to focus on in terms of classroom management. To raise awareness about their own practice, they would also observe in their own classroom before summing up what they wanted to focus on (I). The next step in the process was for the team to reach consensus on what they wanted to develop (G) and then find a common focus for the whole staff (P). The teachers in this school spent a whole semester arriving at a development question they wanted to work on. Helene and Erik both think that it is important to take the time necessary when starting development work so that the teachers are very aware of what they need to develop and are thus motivated to get started. A good start can be the best foundation for further development and may also increase the chances for long-term and lasting learning, Erik believes.

Helene and Erik believe that action learning could be the right method for addressing teachers' learning in the school, seeing this as teachers in teams observing each other in response to focused and specific questions within the framework of the overarching research topic, either connected to the entire school or to each of its three main levels. They are well aware that trust and a good atmosphere among the collaborators is a must for good cooperation and also know that teachers are in a vulnerable situation when they observe each other; they intend to keep this very firmly in mind when they plan and lead the work. Helene and Erik also know that teachers often refrain from challenging each other in conversations after observations, keeping themselves "in the land of nice". They want to try to make the teachers aware of the language that can be used in conversations about observed teaching. The intention is to do this in plenary sessions, but also in reflection conversations held after observing the teaching. In their planning they have decided that Erik should be the one to participate in the observations and reflections with the various teams as he is well liked by his colleagues and will not have a threatening presence in these situations. Helene sees herself as slightly more distanced from the activity in the classroom, but she will also strive to build trust which will eventually allow her to participate constructively in observations and reflections. Helene and Erik also discuss the amount of time they have at their disposal and find that Erik has the most time for this work. Research has told them that the timetable can be an impediment when observation and reflections are part of the development activities, but they are also aware that this approach leads to the biggest changes in classroom practice. They therefore want to enter the time the teachers should spend on observations and reflections into the timetable, but within the timeframe the teachers have at their disposal. This of course means that they will have to discuss the organisation of the development work with the teachers, and they will strive to persuade the teachers to join and support the activity they are proposing. They believe they will succeed on this point as they have research-based knowledge for support. Through mutual observations of their teaching, the teachers will be able to develop networks between classrooms. Helene and Erik also envision linking networks to other schools.

They intend to collaborate with two schools in the vicinity in connection with the development work they are implementing. They hope to collaborate on the leadership level where they exchange ideas on the possibilities and challenges in the work, and where they want teachers to observe and reflect across schools.

Helene and Erik also want to collect data material for analysis as a stage in further development at their school and in this connection list many questions that could help to give direction to the research and acquisition of new and useful knowledge: How did the teachers experience the launch phase of the development work? How do the teachers experience being observed? How do the teachers experience the reflection process after observations? How do the teachers learn? How do they perceive the role of the leaders in the work? How do the teachers experience that the work contributes to changes in practice? Which limitations and possibilities do the teachers see in the work? Which limitations and possibilities do the leader and teacher (that is Erik) see in the work? How do the pupils experience the teaching? How do the teachers and leaders network with the other schools? Is the network collaboration with other schools important for their planning and leading development work?

How important do the teachers find networking with other schools for the teaching practice in their own school? Some of the questions above apply to the on-going development work that Helene and Erik themselves are involved in. For the topics connected to processes they are taking part in, research questions may also surface as the work progresses. They can also ask research questions about on-going work in other schools to improve their knowledge.

Valen school and the development and research work they are planning has been presented above. This is also a training school for student teachers. Having had their practice in the school in the course of their studies, many of the student teachers are about to write their Master's degree thesis and other research assignments. Some of them have told the school that they would like to collect their data in this school because so many exciting things are taking place there. Helene, the principal, has decided that the school can accommodate two of the students, Leander and Leona, and they have sent formal letters to her asking for permission to conduct research. Leander wants to study the collaboration in a teacher team in lower secondary school, preferably Year 9. Leona wants to test a teaching programme in social studies focusing on varied and practical teaching with a teacher who is interested in collaborating on DWR with her. Her research question focuses on how pupils who are struggling with their motivation experience this teaching programme.

3 The Aim of the Book

My intention is that this book will give student teachers, teachers and school leaders research knowledge about which methodologies (research approaches) and methods (data collection and analysis methods) they can use as tools when researching the day-to-day affairs of school and classroom practice. In Chapter 2 I will present CHAT as the framework. When grounded in CHAT the intention of the research will be to produce useful knowledge whether the aim is to promote development when the research is conducted or in coming development processes. The book will thus be useful in connection with DWR, where development work and research are combined in a common project, and in connection with on-going practices in school without the person studying them supporting the on-going development work there and then, but with the intention and understanding that the constructed knowledge can be used in subsequent development processes. The book will also be useful for teacher educators/researchers who supervise student teachers or collaborate with practitioners in schools. Concrete examples will be given as to what could be the focus for research work. In the various chapters I will return to Erik,

Helene, Leander and Leona to see how they can conduct research to develop an understanding of the complexity of leaders' and teachers' cooperation and learning, and to examine the development of the teaching and pupils' learning outcome.

It might be a challenge for student teachers who have not taught in school to carry out DWR in the encounter with experienced leaders and teachers. I will return to his when writing about researcher roles in Chapter 4. In this chapter I describe how it is also possible for the student teachers to carry out DWR. One possible way described, is to be included in a team of teacher educators/researchers collaborating with schools in DWR projects. If student teachers choose to carry out research work without focusing on development in the on-going research, they may still gain insight into how DWR can be carried out through the examples given in this book. This will prepare them for the day-to-day work in school that is on their horizons and show them how they can carry out DWR in the classroom and in collaboration with teachers in the school to develop their own practice and the practice of others. Readers of this book may identify with the possible approaches that are presented and adopt the researcher role that best fits their research project.

4   The Structure of the Book

The book has nine chapters. In the introductory chapter I have brought the reader into a school setting and contextualised it, introducing four people who the reader will meet again in the subsequent chapters. In Chapter 2 I will present different theoretical perspectives with the main focus on CHAT. I will examine the activity system, its origin and development, and how tensions and contradictions are the point of departure for development. I will also present the activity system, the expansive learning circle and the R&D model as the point of departure for research.

In Chapter 3 I will present the historical and theoretical basis for the qualitative methodology and its characteristics. The concepts of ontology, epistemology, methodology and axiology are explained, and issues in research and DWR are presented. The chapter will close with my examination of the researcher's opportunities and challenges.

Chapter 4 describes two researcher roles: the researcher on the sidelines and the researcher in interaction. I also describe how researchers can gain access to the research field, and how they can conduct research in their own or others' context.

Chapter 5 describes different research approaches: case studies, ethnographic studies, phenomenological studies and narrative studies. I examine characteristics of each and look into their goals, data collection and analysis. The chapter also deals with text analysis and conversation analysis.

Data collection is the focus of Chapter 6, where I look at observation and various ways of conducting interviews. For the interview, I will present questions that can be asked in it to obtain confirmation or elaboration of the information that is emerging. The chapter ends with practical advice relating to implementing observations and interviews.

Chapter 7 deals with the constant comparative analysis method, describing the point of departure and purpose of the method, as well as the importance of the theory when the method is applied. The analysis process is exemplified where asking questions and making comparisons are presented as key procedures in the analysis. Furthermore, three key analytical strategies are reviewed in the chapter. In this chapter I also describe how the researchers can study discourse or communication using discourse analyses (D-analyses) to understand how development unfolds.

Chapter 8 focuses on quality and ethics. Knowledge is described as constructed and subjective, and concepts representing quality are examined. The chapter concludes with a review of ethical principles in research.

Chapter 9 looks at writing the Master's thesis itself. First the chapter looks into the content of the introduction to the thesis. Then I explain what thick and thin descriptions are, and look at how the text can be structured. The chapter explores how descriptions may be the point of departure for analyses and how quotations may be embedded in the text. Finally the focus is on how to maintain the flow and cohesion in the thesis.

CHAPTER 2

Theoretical Perspectives and Cultural Historical Activity Theory

1   Different Theoretical Perspectives

In this chapter I will present cultural historical activity theory (CHAT) as a constructivist theory, or more precisely a social constructivist theory. I will explain this particular term later in the chapter. Before addressing CHAT as a theoretical foundation I want to place this theory in relation to other theories. Kuhn (1970) maintains that cognitivism, constructivism and positivism are comprehensive theories, or "paradigms" that cover all other theories and represent different scientific-theory disciplines. They express how we perceive the world, in other words they represent a view of the world. We can look at cognitivism, constructivism and positivism as being on a scale, with cognitivism on one extreme and positivism on the other, and with constructivism between these two. In Figure 2.1 the concepts "mind" and "world" are placed on opposite ends of the scale. Mind relates to cognitivism and world to positivism. The paradigms' perspectives express ideas about how everything is linked and how knowledge can be discovered, and even how new knowledge can be found and created. Hence these theories include ontological, epistemological and methodological perspectives (Denzin & Lincoln, 2011, see Chapter 3 for more about these concepts).

Cognitivism and positivism have both been prominent paradigms in framing research. While we can basically say that these two disciplines are quite the opposite of each other, they both advocate the idea that people do not create or construct the knowledge that eventually becomes part of their own life world. Positivism has been understood as an empirical approach. Learning is seen as a matter of noting and remembering external sensory impressions. The mind may be compared to an empty container, or "tabula rasa". People acquire knowledge through observation and by being lectured to. In the empirical tradition, knowledge is seen as independent of the individual. This view of knowledge is referred to as realism, and the Greek philosopher Aristotle (384-322 BC) is considered to be the founder of this discipline. Behaviourism, as a perspective in positivism, has been the dominant empirical-realistic tradition in the modern history of psychology (Säljö, 1999).

The alternative tradition, the one on the other end of the scale, cognitivism, is often called idealism or rationalism. In this tradition knowledge is understood as the realisation of capacities that lay latent within us. This inherent knowledge that we have been given in our capacity as human beings is activated and emerges with the help of external forces. This help can be teaching in school, or we can gain experience in other ways or through psychological stimulation. The philosopher Plato (428-348 BC) is considered to be the founder of this discipline (Säljö, 1999). The idealist tradition makes a sharp distinction between the real physical world and our knowledge about this reality. Knowledge and skills are considered to be immaterial. What we know and are able to do exists as reflections or images of the world in our intellect. Thus, there is a dividing line between human cognition and the world or surroundings we find ourselves in (Prawat, 1996).

The constructivist paradigm see human beings as active and responsible. Furthermore, knowledge is perceived as a construct of understanding and meaning created in the encounter between people in social interaction. Knowledge is thus not something that is given once and for all and which simply needs to be transferred or realised. On the other hand, knowledge undergoes continuous change and renewal. The constructivist tradition may therefore be seen as building a bridge between people and the world they live in. This means that the social, cultural and historical setting we live in has impact on our perception and understanding. This setting or context thus counteracts pure relativism which would see that everything can mean everything. According to this view, we will be able to more or less share a common understanding within the same context.

Constructivist perspectives are different from both subjective individualism and abstract objectivism. Subjective individualism believes that a human is untouched by the social, cultural and historical context, while abstract objectivism excludes the human interaction factors. Both cognitivist and psychoanalytic theory may be claimed to be prominent representatives of the first-mentioned discipline. Freud believed that a person's perception or understanding is formed according to what he is able to say about himself and his behaviour based on his own internal understanding (Volosinov, 1973). The same understanding is seen in cognitive theory, where development is considered to be a psychological and biological process independent of the social environment (Prawat, 1996). Abstract objectivism, on the other hand, comprises phenomena that exist in the external social world independently of human interference or interaction. The Swiss linguist Ferdinand de Saussure (1857–1913) believed that the structure or system of a language was one such external stable construction independent of changes in the social world (Volosinov, 1973). Hence "the word" is understood as a lexical phenomenon independent of human perception and its use in social interaction. Therefore, applying Saussure's understanding, the word may be perceived as an abstract objective unit, and may consequently also be considered an example within the abstract objectivism tradition. This view contrasts with the way the Russian psychologist Lev S. Vygotsky (1896–1934) and the Russian literary scientist Mikhail M. Bakhtin (1895–1975) see words or utterances (Vygotsky, 2000; Bakhtin, 1981). They claim that words do not exist in any other way than in the context of a person connected to a social setting. This means that the context people live in helps to form and determine the meaning they attach to different words and utterances. Thus words cannot exist as an abstract system and would be meaningless if they were. According to Bakhtin (1986), existence is a dialogic process, which means that there will always be an interaction or interplay between people and between people and the social, cultural and historical world they live in. The different paradigms help to determine which research method the researcher chooses to use. Such a three-part division as I have presented here is a very simple form of classification, but it highlights some important main differences in how we view reality.

Prawat (1996) presented six theories or "theoretical models" which can be placed on a scale ranging between people and the world they live in, between "mind" and "world". The theoretical models will then lie on this scale between cognitivism and positivism. These theories are Piaget's schema theory, Mead's symbolic interactionism, Dewey's idea-based constructivism, socio-cultural theory (Vygotsky, 1978, 2000; Wertsch, 1991, 1998; Cole, 1996), social constructionism (Gergen, 1995; Rorty, 1989) and finally information processing theory (Mayer, 1996). Inspired by Prawat, I have developed Figure 2.1.

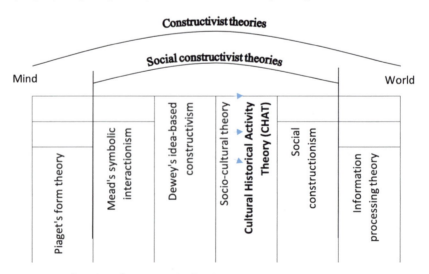

FIGURE 2.1   Overview of constructivist theories

CHAT, which develops the theory of Vygotsky has been called socio-cultural theory in the West. As we see from Figure 2.1, Prawat (1996) defines socio-cultural theory as social constructivist theory. Hence CHAT is also called social constructivism. In this chapter I will examine CHAT in more detail.

2   Cultural Historical Activity Theory

Both socio-cultural theory and CHAT have started from Marxist perspectives, which implies building a bridge or an interaction between the person and the world he or she lives in. The philosopher and social economist Karl Marx (1818–1883) believed that material circumstances had impact on the norms, beliefs and values of people. A fundamental feature in his theory was his understanding that human perception was anchored in history and the material conditions people live under. In his theory, how people see themselves and the world is a product of the real conditions they live under. Thus the perspectives of meaning may vary with the material conditions (Volosinov, 1973).

As the development of CHAT has been based on Vygotsky's theories, the view which emerges in CHAT can also be found in socio-cultural theory. However, the first key characteristic feature of CHAT was developed by Leont'ev (Wertsch, 1981). This first feature refers to analysing activity on three levels; the activity, action and operation levels. Different activities are discerned according to the object for the activity, and the motive for the actions is in the activity itself. The object can be material or idealistic. It may be a lump of clay you are trying to shape into a nice vase or communication you are trying to develop with your pupils, or this latter point may be the overarching goal, for example, for a teacher team. An activity consists of different actions that are coordinated to move it towards the object. Each action represents intermediate steps to satisfy the motive for the activity. In a teacher team this implies that each member carries out different actions which together will lead them in the direction of a common object. Each team in a school may work towards goals which together lead all the activities in the school towards the collective goal in the organisation.

Moreover, the actions are carried out under different circumstances where aids are available (Leont'ev, 1981). The goal-directed actions is the second feature of CHAT. The third characteristic is that these actions are mediated. All local activities have a connection to historically and culturally formed artefacts which mediate action (Wertsch, 1981). The mediating artefacts contribute to forming and creating the activity in a special way. They are combined, used and transformed in new ways in a local common activity. A key understanding in Vygotsky's theory and CHAT is that learning first occurs on a social level (inter-mental level), then is internalised (intra-mental level) (Vygotsky, 1978). All higher mental functions are perceived as having a social and cultural origin which emerges from "the general genetic law of cultural development" (Vygotsky, 1978, p. 57). Human beings are perceived as being active in the learning process, and language is an important mediating artefact in learning processes. Language is seen as "the tool above all tools" (Luria, 1928; Vygotsky, 2000). Vygotsky's focus was to start with the learning of the child, but his ideas have also been applied in the context of teachers' learning and development (Postholm, 2012, 2018a; Postholm & Wæge, 2015).

As in socio-cultural theory, development is important on several levels in CHAT, and this is the fourth characteristic of this theory (Wertsch, 1981). This may apply to the development of the individual, a team or the genetic development of a species, and it can include development in a historical perspective. The fifth trait is also closely connected to development processes. CHAT expresses that human activity and the means by which it is mediated have come about in social interaction. The sixth and seventh traits are precisely about learning processes in social interaction. These are called internalisation and externalisation. Internalisation is related to reproduction of the culture within which the actions take place. Externalisation refers to the processes that create new artefacts or new ways of applying them. In a team, this may mean how team members develop and test teaching methods which each of them eventually can start to use. The expansive learning cycle visualises the internalisation and externalisation processes (Engeström, 1987, 2001). I will deal with this learning cycle later in the chapter.

A research approach has been developed in CHAT that has been called developmental work research (DWR) (Engeström & Engeström, 1986). The intention of research using CHAT as its theoretical underpinning is to produce new action-oriented knowledge, not "true" knowledge in a universal sense. In Norway the term R&D work (research and development work) is used, but as the theory foundation here is CHAT, I will use the term DWR. DWR is a "formative intervention" (Engeström & Sannino, 2010) methodology that promotes positive change in practices using a participatory, collaborative design. The researcher is called a "formative interventionist researcher". The role of teacher educators as formative interventionist researchers is to provoke and sustain an expansive transformation process led and owned by the school leaders and teachers (Engeström & Sannino, 2010). This type of researcher conducts research together with practitioners, as when creating and using mirror data (Cole & Engeström, 2007) and functioning as a collective mirror for the participants, as Engeström (2000) puts it. The researcher can also introduce a model (the activity system presented below) practitioners can use to analyse how the practice has been, how it is and how it can be changed in the future. Furthermore, the researchers can present ideas and tools as mediating artefacts to help the practitioners to see and help them develop new practices (Engeström, 2007). In this way different perspectives can mesh when deciding what the focus for the development should be.

CHAT is both a theory and a method which sees the importance of developing collective systems. Research in CHAT sees people as systems within systems of social relations. This means, for example, that research can be focused on the school as an organisation, or that the researcher can zoom in on individual factors in the organisation, such as a teacher team. The teacher team, however, is analysed and understood as part of the school's holistic system. I will return to this when I present the activity system as an analytical unit. Within the CHAT context I will present models that can be used in development processes, and I will suggest which methodologies may be applied when researching the development processes. As I have described above, the researcher may assume a role where he or she supports the development processes while also researching them. Erik will assume this researcher role in his school. He will also undertake research on processes that have taken place in his school and in the network of schools they collaborate with, and thus carry out more traditional qualitative research. Later in the chapter I will propose which qualitative studies researchers can conduct for research on development processes.

3 The Activity System: Its Origin and Development

Vygotsky (1978) described a situation where sheets of paper were positioned to help a man move from point A to point B. To start with, these sheets of paper can be seen as neutral objects placed on the floor. Once a person starts to actively use these sheets of paper to help him get to point B, they become aids for carrying out this action. The task was to move from A to B, where the task was the stimulus (S) intended to trigger a response (R). Functions that are called "natural" or unmediated are those that appear through the baseline of an upside-down triangle (the S-R line) (see Figure 2.2). This represents the actions carried out without the person using any aids. These actions follow the biological or natural development line in humans, representing the behaviourist understanding. These are elementary actions which may be considered direct human reactions to a stimulus (Vygotsky, 1978). Two lines going from each end of the baseline form the top vertex in this upside-down triangle. The top vertex represents the aids humans can actively apply to help them carry out the task. The action is thus not a direct response to the task, but a conscious action where available aids are used, representing a social constructivist perspective on human activity, learning and development. Vygotsky's (1978) upside-down triangle is presented in Figure 2.2.

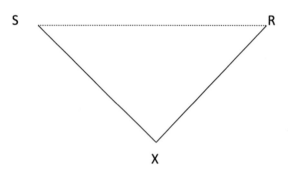

FIGURE 2.2   Vygotsky's triangle showing the intermediate stage between stimulus and response via X, an aid

Based on this triangle, CHAT has been developed graphically into what is called the activity system (Engeström, 1987, 2001). In this activity system, Vygotsky's triangle is represented in the uppermost triangle but is turned around so that the top vertex is now uppermost. Whereas CHAT has been developed from Vygotsky's theories, the activity system is a graphic development of CHAT (Engeström, 1987, 2001). In the collective activity system human activity is structured and visualised by several triadic relations, and the system functions as an analytical unit for the activity that is to be developed and studied (Engeström, 1987, 1999, 2001). This system is visualised in Figure 2.3.

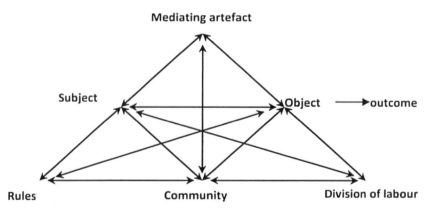

FIGURE 2.3   The activity system

The upper triangle in the activity system is the same as Vygotsky's (1978) fundamental triangle, but, as mentioned, it is turned upside down with the mediating artefacts at the top (see Figure 2.3). The concept of mediated action or cultural mediation that is the key point in socio-cultural theory advances Vygotsky's theory that the individual's mental activity is founded on and integrated in a mutually social, cultural, educational and historical context (Wertsch, 1991, 1998). The minimum elements of an activity system include subject, mediating artefacts (signs and tools), object, rules, community and division of labour (Engeström, 1987, 2001).

Mediated actions are integrated in the system in the upper triangle. Mediating artefacts function as intermediary aids which the acting subject chooses to use when trying to attain the goals for the actions. The system shows the close connection between the acting subject, which can either be an individual or a group of people (Engeström, 1999), and the context. Context is not reduced to something that just surrounds, but is interwoven in the actions, becoming a single process. The actions exist only in relation to the context that is visualised by the three triangles at the bottom of the activity system (Cole, 1996). The context that comprises the factors rules, community and division of labour determines the premises and also any restrictions for the subject's goal-directed actions.

Rules include norms and conventions that direct the actions in the activity system. The factor community refers to all people who share the same goals. Division of labour means that the work or the goal-directed actions are divided between and conducted by people belonging to the community. The concept division of labour makes it possible to distinguish between collective activity and individual action (Engeström, 1987; Cole, 1996; Engeström & Miettinen, 1999). When people divide work between themselves, each their own result does not satisfy their needs. Rather their needs are satisfied by the portion of the product of their aggregate activity that they gain in their social relation during the working process. The activity system as a unit of analysis makes the system view and the subject's view complementary factors that can be analysed in relation to each other (Engeström & Miettinen, 1999). The factor division of labour makes it possible to distinguish between collective activity and individual action. This represents the horizontal work division. The roles can also be divided vertically, which can also reveal the power perspective in a team or school staff.

3.1   Tensions and Contradictions as the Basis for Development

The view in CHAT is that tensions or contradictions in and between activity systems are the starting point for change and development (Engeström & Sannino, 2010). These may be "tensions or contradictions in factors". If a teacher team is defined as the acting subject in the activity system, some of the team members might want change, while others might prefer stability. The tensions in a factor are called "primary contradictions". "Secondary contradictions", that is "tensions or contradictions between factors", can also arise in the activity system. One example may be that the teachers in the team, as the acting subject, do not quite agree on how the object for the activity should be designed. Another tension or contradiction might be that the team does not feel they have sufficient aids to satisfy the object they have decided to work on. There may also be "tension or contradiction between the new and the remains of the old practice" in an organisation, which is referred to as "tertiary contradictions". When two or more schools collaborate in a network to develop common practice, there may also be "tensions or contradictions between the schools as activity systems". There may be disagreement relating to which object they want to focus on. There may also be contradictions about which aids they would like to use to help them move towards the object for the activity. There may also be tensions or contradictions between a teacher training institution and a school. This tension could be based on schools feeling that they are not getting the assistance they would like to have from the university teacher education staff, or that teacher educators find that leaders and teachers in the school are not aware of the needs they have for support in their development processes. These are called "quaternary contradictions". When tensions or contradictions are solved or eliminated, change and development occur, according to Engeström and Miettinen (1999).

The activity system may provide good help when the activity in a school is to be analysed to uncover tensions or contradictions with the aim of creating and implementing measures. A teacher, a team and a staff can then decide which topic they would like to work with when they have found a contradiction between the current and the desired practices. The other factors in the activity system will then be analysed in relation to the object and according to the chosen issue. As the activity system is dynamic, a new object will impact the other factors in the system. The object for Valen school may be: "Develop the communication between teachers and between teachers and pupils to promote academic and relational development".

To visualise mediated actions in a DWR project Engeström (2001) has developed the expansive learning cycle. Expansive learning is defined as "learning something that is not yet there" (Engeström & Sannino, 2010, p. 2). This may refer to developing new structures for collaboration in a team, such as making it possible for teachers to observe and mutually reflect on their teaching to help them develop communication with each other and in dialogue with the pupils so that the teachers learn more. A new practice with focus on communication may also help the teachers to develop their learning culture so that the practice community becomes a learning community. With these structural and cultural changes they can also develop their communication with the pupils and the relations between themselves and between them and the pupils. The teachers in the team and the staff may then move in the zone of proximal development, defined within a collective and social perspective (Engeström, 1987). Engeström (1987) has developed Vygotsky's (1978) individual definition of the zone of proximal development, writing: "It is the distance between the present everyday actions of the individuals and the historically new form of the societal activity that can be collectively generated [...]" (p. 174). This means that both the activity and the culture in the communication are developed and changed. This can apply to activity in a team or the school as a whole. The expansive learning cycle (Engeström, 1987, 2001) is presented in Figure 2.4.

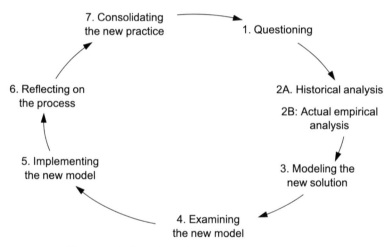

FIGURE 2.4   The expansive learning cycle

The object in this example is to develop the communication between teachers and between teachers and pupils to promote subject and relational development so that there is greater learning outcome from the teaching. A good development question could then be "How can the communication in the encounter with teachers and between teachers and pupils be developed so that the pupils' learning outcome and the relationships between all the parties involved are improved?" Formulating the development question for the object is the first step on the expansive learning cycle (1). The next step in the cycle is to carry out historical and present-time analyses (2). To understand the quality of the collaboration between the teachers in the school and how they have communicated with each other and with the pupils, the teachers can observe both themselves and each other to understand the current situation. They can also reflect together on the quality of the communication and relationships in the school. When the teachers find that they know the current situation and its history, they can start to develop a new model or solution (new content in the factors in the activity system) to promote the collective practice in school in terms of communication and relationships. After new content has been placed in the different factors in the activity system or model (3), the new solution/model (4) is analysed to find possible outcomes the solution or model can lead to when it is used. In the phase after the solution or model has been analysed, and prior to implementation, the teachers can use small tests with focused questions where the development question serves as the framework. A question for a class or a teaching period could be "How do I give the pupils feedback in the teaching that will help them to progress in solving their assignments?" Thus, small innovative learning circles are tested before the new practice is implemented. These innovative circles could be left as single events without becoming expansive, while other small innovative learning circles together can represent the new solution, which thereafter will be implemented and thus put to work (5). Thus a new collective practice has also been developed. The teachers learn from their experiences, which is called action learning (Revans, 1982, 1984).

Thus, teachers can develop their practice in their own classrooms by examining their teaching from the researcher's perspective. The action learning of teachers (Postholm & Jacobsen, 2011) is visualised in the Figure 2.5:

The teachers critically examine their own teaching using the development question as the framework. In action learning they collect information to illuminate and hopefully answer the questions. This information can then be used to improve the situation. Measures are implemented and tested, and then in turn are made the object of continuous analysis and reflection, while what the teachers experience and perceive is assessed according to theories from the field. This in turn forms the basis for new curiosity, new questions and new measures. Thus learning can take place in a continuous process, as shown by the action learning circle. As mentioned above, these innovative circles may constitute single events without becoming expansive, while other small innovative learning circles together can represent the new solution for the teaching practice for the team or the whole school.

After the new solution/model has been implemented (5), the teachers reflect in teams, and in the next instance in the whole staff, where the leader should also attend, on how the solution/model works in practice (6). If they find that the solution works, the tests of individual teams could be merged into a holistic plan which eventually will be consolidated in practice (7). In

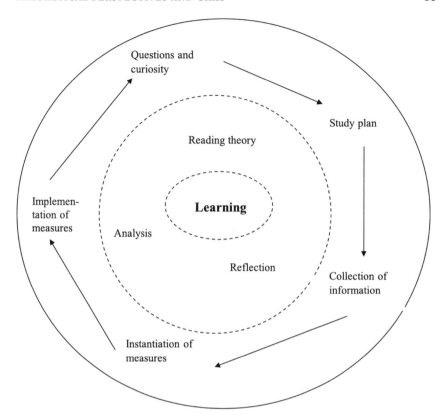

FIGURE 2.5   The action learning circle

the development processes in Valen school it will be important that Erik and Helene allocate time so that the teachers can agree on what they want to implement as a new common practice in the school or the teams. After this a new focus and new tests with new development questions can be introduced.

The activity system and the expansive learning cycle may be good tools for leaders and teachers when they, as researchers, are to promote change and development in school. Researchers invited to join teams and schools may also use these models in the dialogue with teachers and leaders to analyse and develop the activity and its context.

4   Researching Development Processes

4.1   *The Activity System as the Point of Departure for Research*
When carrying out research in CHAT and using the activity system as the unit of analysis, the focus may be on tensions in and between factors in the activity

system, and on tertiary and quaternary tensions. In addition, the research may focus on specific activities when teachers take action in the school. The following paragraphs will exemplify this. The research approaches proposed are described in Chapter 5.

When the researcher studies tensions or contradictions within a factor, a research question when focusing on the factor "subject" could be: "How are the teachers in the Year 8 team motivated for development activities?" When answering this question the researcher can describe and explain why some teachers are more motivated than others. Some may want more stability than others who want to change the practice in the school. A NARRATIVE STUDY can contribute knowledge about this difference and explain it.

Another focus may be on the factor "division of labour". Do the teachers want to work individually, or do they want to work collectively? The answer to this question can show whether there is a culture or collective responsibility in school so that the teachers develop their practice and learn together. A MICRO-ETHNOGRAPHIC STUDY can answer this. Community includes both teachers and leaders in the school. A research study could for example identify whether the school leaders support the teachers and whether they agree and are motivated to act on the same object. Teacher educators may be considered a mediating artefact in school-based professional development. The language used in presentations and in dialogues with teachers and school leaders is a mediating artefact in the development processes. Both MICRO-ETHNOGRAPHIC and PHENOMENOLOGICAL STUDIES can be used to understand the processes and how they are experienced. CONVERSATION ANALYSIS can also be used to analyse the dialogue between teacher educators and teachers and leaders. D-analysis, that I present in Chapter 7, is also used to analyse language use with the intention to study development. I do not suggest D-analysis throughout the chapter, because I perceive it as a method of analyses and not as a methodology.

An interesting question which focuses on the relationship between factors in the activity system can put the focus on the relationship between the subject and object factors, and the dialogues between the subjects that are related to the object. Leont'ev (1978) wrote: "[...] The object of the activity is twofold: first, in its independent existence as subordinating to itself and transforming the activity of the subject, second; as an image of the object, as product of its property of psychological reflection that is realised as an activity of the subject" (p. 52). The object may thus be material or ideal. As I exemplified above, the object could be a lump of clay and its properties that you are attempting to shape into a nice vase, or the object could be a teacher team developing communication with pupils.

In a national programme implemented in all lower secondary schools in Norway, the object was determined by the authorities (Ministry of Education and Research, 2011, 2012) and applied to all national efforts. The focus for the programme in lower secondary school had to be on classroom management, writing, reading or numeracy. This means that the object transformed the activity of the subject, as change in one factor in the activity system creates something new in the dynamic system. The subjects could, however, decide *what* they wanted to develop within the framework of these topics. In such national programmes for school where the object has been determined by the authorities it is therefore necessary to initiate a dialogue between all the practitioners in school, both leaders and teachers, so that they can develop a common object to work on. In this way the common object may become the "product of its property of psychological reflection that is realised as an activity of the subject" (Leont'ev, 1978, p. 52). According to Leont'ev (1981), "the object is the true motive" for people's actions (p. 59). Similarly, according to Cole and Engeström (2007), teachers' motivation can be built into the object because it is their practice and needs that serve as the starting point. This can be the case if teachers are allowed to help decide what should be developed in school. The dialogue that takes place when an object is formed may be an interesting research focus. Studies may devote attention to both culture and opinions related to the dialogue taking place. Thus both MICRO-ETHNOGRAPHIC STUDIES and PHENOMENOLOGICAL STUDIES can be relevant. A tension or contradiction can also arise between rules presented in white papers and national curricula, and objects designed by practitioners in school. In this context political documents can be analysed (TEXT ANALYSIS) in relation to objects developed in school by leaders and teachers.

As mentioned above, tertiary and quaternary contradictions can be the point of departure for research. A research question may focus on contradictions between a recently established activity and what is left from the previous way of conducting the activity. Engeström and Sannino (2010) explain that quaternary activities are contradictions between a recently organised activity and its proximal activity system. There may be contradictions between the current activity system, one that has existed for years, for example between teacher education institutions and schools which cooperate on developing the practice in both arenas. Such a contradiction may block the developmental transfer between the involved parties (Engeström & Sannino, 2010). MICRO-ETHNOGRAPHIC STUDIES and PHENOMENOLOGICAL STUDIES can address a research focus related to this.

The mediating artefact is what transforms the object to the outcome. The outcome can be ideal or material, or both. In school the ultimate goal is that the pupils should learn and develop. Both teachers and pupils may have an idea about what they have learnt. The research question and the study can then be designed to make sense of the experiences of both the teachers' and the pupils' learning. PHENOMENOLOGICAL STUDIES could thus be carried out with teachers and pupils to gain an understanding of their learning. Moreover, tests and written assignments can be included in the material to ascertain what the pupils have learnt.

4.2 The Expansive Learning Cycle and the R&D Model as the Starting Point for Research

Research carried out in and between activity systems may contribute knowledge about the status before and after goal-directed actions have been implemented. With the expansive learning cycle and the R&D model (presented below) as the point of departure, mediated actions will be in focus, but the now-situation will also be in focus in addition to how the practice has been at the school at the time the development activity is started. A researcher can study how teachers formulate a question that is intended to set the direction for or frame development processes, and he or she can study how teachers carry out historical and current empirical analyses. For Erik, this will mean researching the processes he initiates to prepare development questions, and he must obtain data to understand how the situation has been and still is in terms of the issues the school wants to focus on. All the steps in the expansive learning cycle can be the focus for the research. To study development processes MICRO-ETHNOGRAPHIC STUDIES and PHENOMENOLOGICAL STUDIES can be used, but also CASE STUDIES, which are studies of a bounded system (Creswell, 2013) in time and place, such as the teaching sessions the teachers plan for single classes and for longer periods of time. Leona can set a case study in motion where she examines the teaching programmes she wants to test. This could also be a study of a teacher team over a particular period of time focusing on how the team members develop the language in their dialogue to promote the teaching practice. When studying a team, Erik can carry out a CONVERSATION ANALYSIS to study the dialogue between the teachers, or he can choose to conduct a MICRO-ETHNOGRAPHIC STUDY to examine the learning culture in the team.

In connection with pupils' learning it is expected that they should develop a meta-cognitive competence and become self-regulated in the learning process (Boekaerts, Pintrich, & Zeidner, 2000; Flavell, 1979, 1987; Pintrich, 2000; Zimmerman, 2006). For this reason it should be expected that teachers have a meta-cognitive attitude to their own learning and development. This thinking is embedded in the R&D model (Postholm & Moen, 2011) presented in Figure 2.6.

THEORETICAL PERSPECTIVES AND CHAT

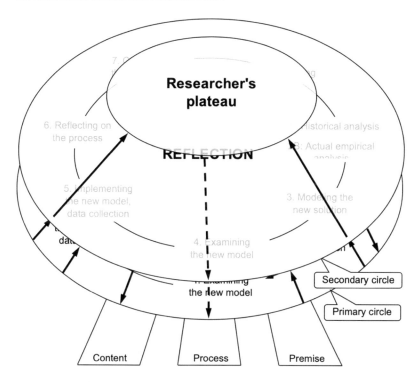

FIGURE 2.6   The R&D model

The expansive learning cycle in this model is called the "primary circle" because it is the circle that gives direction to the development processes (Postholm & Moen, 2011). The circle above it, called the "secondary circle", represents the researchers', in this case Erik, and the teachers' joint reflections on the processes that have taken place and are presented in the primary circle. For example, the following may be the focus of the reflection: How did the researcher and the teachers arrive at the development question? How do they undertake analyses in relation to the past and the present? How do they plan the teaching programmes, and how do they analyse them? How do they implement the plan and programmes? How do they collect data material during the implementation phase, and how do they systematically reflect afterwards on how their plan can be applied in practice, looking at whether it needs to be developed, or should it simply be dropped? Coghlan and Brannick (2005) claim that this second level is the researchers' domain, but in my view the researcher's job is also to raise the teachers up to this level. A two-way relation between action and reflection is illustrated with the arrows going both ways between the primary and secondary circles. When the teachers reflect on the reflections they made in the primary circle, meta-learning will also occur. As I see it, it is necessary to include the premises for the actions, the content and the processes that have been present in all the reflection processes. This means understanding what is happening in its context.

The model also features a third level which is called the "researcher's plateau". This illustrates a level with no direct collaboration between researchers and teachers and leaders. It is a transparent level from which the researchers can focus their researcher's eye. The focus may therefore be somewhat narrow, which implies that topics can be studied that are not necessarily included in phases represented in the primary and secondary circles. I (Postholm, 2008a, 2008b) have formulated research questions from this plateau as the framework for studies. I did not think of these problem formulations prior to the start of the DWR but developed them according to the processes as they progressed. They resulted in two texts with different focus points. One focused on the launch phase and the other on actions and reflections. I (Postholm, 2008a) had not foreseen that the first semester would become a specific phase in the work, or that this launch phase would become the foundation on which the further work was built, nor that reflections would be as important as they were.

According to Vygotsky (1997), the development of the research question and the method occurs, if not parallel to each other, then at least by taking shape in accordance with each other. The method thus becomes simultaneously a necessity and a product, a tool and a result of the research. This means that research questions may be developed during the research process, and that the researcher must also be open to carrying out research in other ways than initially intended. What is quite certain is that Erik is not familiar with the processes in his school and does not know how they will unfold. It is therefore highly probable that a research focus he has not considered will surface during the ongoing work.

I have now presented CHAT with the activity system and the expansive learning cycle as tools in research activities in school. The activity system and the expansive learning cycle can be good tools for the leader who is fronting change and development activities together with the teachers. Researchers or external resource persons invited into teams and schools may also use these models in the dialogue with teachers and leaders to analyse and develop the activity and its context in the school.

CHAPTER 3

The Qualitative Method: Its Historical and Theoretical Roots and Characteristics

1   Introduction

In this chapter I will present the history of the qualitative method, starting with studies which have a focus on exploring "the other" and moving on to the researcher as a participant in the field during the research who is supporting the processes. I will also present the theoretical foundation of qualitative research before I examine different ways a researcher can approach the research field. This will be followed by a presentation of the special features of the method and then I will conclude by looking at the challenges and opportunities that come with this researcher role.

2   Historical Roots

When using the qualitative method the intention is to understand and describe what specific individuals do in their day-to-day lives and the meaning their actions have for them. Description, understanding and meaning are key concepts in a text presenting a qualitative study. To begin with, the main purpose of qualitative research has been to describe and understand "the other", referring most often to people from another culture than the researcher, an Indian tribe, for example, or an immigrant minority group. The Latin word "qualitas" refers to having the primary focus on qualities or features of different phenomena, what makes them different. "Quantitas" refers to having the main focus on differences in amount (Erickson, 2011). It is important for the qualitative researcher to produce "thick descriptions" (Geertz, 1973) so that the differences and similarities can be clearly illuminated in the qualitative text presenting the research findings.

When describing the history of the qualitative method, my main source is Frederick Erickson's chapter in *Handbook of Qualitative Research* (Denzin & Lincoln, 2011, pp. 43–59) and Erickson's chapter in *Handbook of Research on Teaching* (Wittrock, 1986, pp. 119–161). The roots of qualitative research can be traced all the way back to antiquity. The Greek scholar Herodotus, who wrote in the 500s BC, had an interest in history across cultures. During the Renaissance and Baroque periods reports about everyday practices were given in "how to" books, including a book on how to improvise when playing music. Descriptive reports were also produced about the situation of native Americans under Spanish colonial rule in the 1600s. Then as now there was tension between the scope of the study and how specific and unique the description should be.

At around the same time that writers began to describe the practices of everyday life, the quantitative physics of Galileo Galilei and Isaac Newton were also being established. Quantitative studies became the standard for natural science during the Enlightenment. The goal was to find general laws that could apply to everything in the physical world and to causal relations that would be universal. Attempts were made in France and Germany to generalise social processes according to analyses of frequency data. Some of the French Enlightenment philosophers in the eighteenth century attempted to mathematically model social processes.

Stories about people's everyday lives were still published in this era, but the focus in these published stories eventually changed. In the sixteenth and seventeenth centuries the lower social classes were described in a condescending way. Towards the end of the eighteenth century, however, these groups were described in a more sympathetic way. Pierre Beaumarchais's play *The Wedding of Figaro*, written in 1778, is an example of this. Because the play favoured servants and described the aristocratic characters in the play satirically, it was at first banned in both Paris and Vienna. At the end of the nineteenth century the brothers Grimm collected stories from German peasants, and in Norway Asbjørnsen and Moe collected folk tales and legends that became an important element in the exploration of Norwegian identity in the nineteenth century. Documentation of folklore and the lives of ordinary people became a general practice.

By the mid nineteenth century attempts were made to systematically define studies of social life. A fundamental disagreement developed about which branch of science the social sciences should come under. Some thought that sociological studies should be practised in the same way as in natural science, as the philosophers during the Enlightenment had hoped would be the case. The sociologist Auguste Comte (1822/2001) proposed that statistics should be used when studying social life. At this time many anthropologists also wanted to generalise their findings, for example by developing an understanding of how a cultural and physical human being has changed in universal steps over time, from the barbarian to contemporary man (Erickson, 2011).

On the other hand, the German philosopher Wilhelm Dilthey believed in an approach that differed from natural science (which he called Naturwissenschaften). He believed in carrying out social studies as Geisteswissenschaften, human science, human studies or humanities. This approach was common during the final half of the nineteenth century in the humanities and what we now call the social sciences. The focus here was on meaning and actions connected to everyday life. The aim of the studies was to develop understanding rather than proof and hypotheses or predictions. Dilthey has influenced a number of younger scientists, such as Max Weber, the philosophical phenomenologists Edmund Husserl and Martin Heidegger, the hermeneutic Hans-Georg Gadamer and the anthropologist Clifford Geertz (Erickson, 2011).

At the end of the nineteenth century anthropologists started calling anthropology ethnography (Erickson, 2011). Anthropology aimed to develop understanding across cultures, while ethnography aimed to understand one culture (Wolcott, 2008). According to Erickson (2011), manuals were developed for observations and interviews in the first studies. The goal was to accurately collect data and provide detailed descriptions of the lives of the subjects being studied. These studies generally examined other cultures than those the researchers lived in. People in colonies or Indian tribes would be "put under the microscope". Even if the intention in the initial ethnographic studies was to "write about the other", it would often be the researcher's perspective (etic) and not the other's perspective (emic) that was highlighted. I will return to these perspectives later in the chapter.

In his study *Argonauts of the Western Pacific* Bronislaw Malinowski (1922) claimed that he had conducted a study and presented it in such a way that it described the perspective of the participants, the emic perspective. His research was carried out on the Trobriand islands in Melanesia, a colony under British rule, during WW1. Malinowski was a Polish student at the University of Oxford, but he was suspected of being a spy by the island authorities and was therefore detained there. Malinowski remained on these islands for such a long time that he believed that he was able to put into words the lives of the people living there better than they could do themselves. The anthropologist Kluckhohn (1949) states in an aphorism that the fish is the last to discover the water. Bearing this statement in mind, it could be said that the inhabitants of these islands were the ones who had lost sight of the familiar; only the researcher who came from other surroundings or another culture could use his outsider view to see or discover what for them was so trivial that it could not be grasped by sight, language or thought.

Many anthropologists believed that Malinowski's ethnography was too subjective and hence too unscientific. Other researchers, however, were enthusiastic about his way of conducting research. Malinowski's approach to research and how it was presented is consistent with the psycho-analytical perspective of Sigmund Freud (1856–1939). This perspective claims that people are unable to express or find words for everything they know. Freud's perspective was also consistent with the broad intellectual and artistic environment in expressionism, a direction in art which lasted from the end of the nineteenth century to around 1940. The term expressionism of course stems from the verb "to express". Expressionist painters were not really interested in reproducing reality as it actually was. For them it was important to paint what they felt about the surrounding world, highlighting emotions, moods and thoughts. It was not important for the expressionists to highlight details in the paintings. They would paint with coarse brushes, with visible brush strokes and colours applied in thick layers. These artists were most interested in using strong colours in their own way so there is no guarantee that the sea is blue and the sun yellow in their paintings. The sea could just as well be purple and the sun red (Lynton, 1980).

Malinowski the ethnographer was interested in how the cultural and social surroundings coloured the inner life of people, and he wanted to describe people's lives as seen from their perspectives (Erickson, 1986). Malinowski's research has later come under criticism based both on diaries he kept during his research and a review of his research on the inhabitants of these islands who remembered Malinowski's presence. They did not recognise themselves in all the descriptions that were presented. The diaries also showed asymmetry between Malinowski and the people he studied. For example, he wrote in his diary that he disliked them and that he longed for civilisation.

In 1928 the ethnographer Margaret Mead published her study entitled *Coming of Age in Samoa*. She has been criticised for being too naïve, for believing too much in what the informants told her. Others felt that the informants simply told her what she wanted to hear. Their upbringing, Mead wrote, was not as turbulent as that of American children. Some have also remarked that Mead's analyses were correct. In response to this criticism participatory action research or collaborative action research emerged. In this research, analyses are tested during the research itself in the field where it has been conducted (Erickson, 2011).

Starting in the 1950s qualitative research has also been conducted in schools (see for example Spindler, 1955). Teaching was studied and presented in narrative research texts. In the early 1990s, qualitative research also became common in humanities subjects and natural science subjects, such as mathematics. From the origin of the qualitative method its intention was, as mentioned above, to describe "the other". This is still the case, but it is also accepted that the researcher's experiences will influence what is being studied and how the collected material is understood. Today it is also assumed that the research participants will read the research text or parts of it, and that they may also contribute as co-authors. In addition to conducting research on processes, researchers can also take part in supporting their development (Erickson, 1986, 2011), as in DWR.

Erik has also been thinking that the teachers in his school should be co-authors for texts they write after he has finished his Master's thesis. In the research for this thesis he intends to be aware of his own position, his own subjectivity, by dwelling on his experiences and perceptions and the theories that may colour his researcher's eye. He is aware that the theories he is reading will help to point him in the direction of what he is looking for and influence how he analyses and understands things. Indeed, he is also aware of how these theories will also cloud his researcher's gaze. Thus Erik will carry with him both scientific theories and subjective individual theories in his research. The process whereby the researcher reflects on his own role as researcher and hence his own subjectivity in interaction with the research participants and with the topics in focus is called the reflexive process (Altheide & Johnson, 2011; Glesne, 2011; Kvale & Brinkmann, 2015; Lincoln & Guba, 2000).

3   Theoretical Roots

In Chapter 2 I presented paradigms which express each their view of the world. It is my belief that qualitative research in general is within the constructivist perspective, which means that knowledge is created in the encounter with the researcher and the research field. Above I have described how Erik brings his prior knowledge into the research where new knowledge is developed. I have mentioned "paradigms" for comprehensive theories and constructivist theories for "theoretical models". I have presented social constructivist theories in Figure 2.1. These are general theories which express how individuals are perceived and how knowledge is created. These theories then branch out to theories that build on empirical data, and which thus have strong ties to concrete processes in everyday life, for example in school. Called "intermediate theories" (Merton, 1967), they are often represented by concepts. Such theories are for example Dewey's (1916) theory of experiential learning and Vygotsky's (1978) theory of the zone of proximal development. Both Dewey and Vygotsky conducted research in which they studied these concepts in practical activities. These theories have therefore been closely connected to the real world.

Comprehensive theories, theoretical models and intermediate theories give direction to research and research questions, moving ever closer to the practice field. "Substantive theories" are the most restricted theory type, forming the foundation for concrete and researchable problem areas. In a DWR project they may also form the foundation for development questions and for knowledge-based development. Substantive theories are connected to people at a particular time in a specific context. These theories are thus developed according to studies of a concrete and local action, and will therefore be easily identifiable (Gudmundsdottir, 1992). For example, these theories could refer to how leaders lead development work, how teachers work in teams, how learning processes are planned, how the classroom management is, how pupil cooperation is and how pupils are guided in the teaching. Even if these theories are limited to specific contexts and situations, it is a challenge to settle on focused research questions. What should be in focus in development processes when, for example, teachers are to develop their classroom management skills will also depend on the allocated time for the work. This will help the teachers to agree on where in the field their attention should be placed. An overview of the theories mentioned above is presented in Figure 3.1.

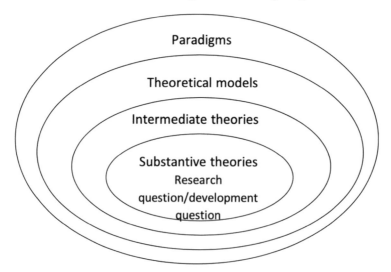

FIGURE 3.1   Overview of theories on different levels

Even if theories give the study its framework and direction, the qualitative researcher is fully present in the research. This means that the perceptions and experiences of the researcher, as well as the theories he or she has read, has impact on the research and the research findings. The qualitative researcher is the most important research instrument throughout the entire research process (Creswell, 2013), and the researcher's subjective individual theories will therefore be highly important in both research and DWR projects. How the researcher's subjective and individual theories can influence the researcher in his or her work is described in words and pictures below.

3.1 Subjective, Individual Theories

Figure 3.2, as I see it, shows a vase, a serving plate or two people facing each other. This is basically an interplay between the colours white and black, but we see a vase or an attractive serving plate because we have seen similar vases or serving plates before. We are well acquainted with faces so we can also see these in the picture, if we are able to shake the idea of a vase or serving plate out of our minds.

FIGURE 3.2
A vase, a serving plate and two faces

What we see depends on what we have seen previously and thus are able to relate to the picture. Our previous experiences will similarly colour what we see and how we experience, thus also what will be the dominant focus of our research.

During the impressionist period series paintings were developed, where Monet was especially interested in this way of painting. For example, he would paint haystacks under the light of the day during which he was painting as well under the shifting lights of the seasons. Impressionists also focused on atmospheric moods, such as vapour, searing sunlight and fog, which would give their motif different expressions. We can also use this example in the sphere of research. A situation in one setting may be perceived in different ways by different researchers, depending on which theories, perceptions and experiences they bring into their research. Two researchers carried out studies with the same focus in a classroom with the same teacher, but the resultant narratives differed. Perhaps surprisingly, the teacher in focus felt that both the narratives were true. The knowledge that was constructed between the researchers and the research participant was different because their interaction and what the researcher brought into the research field differed (Gudmundsdottir, 2001). This is supported by Shulman (1981), who also points out that different researchers and authors may lead to different interpretations and presentations. Thus, based on what I have presented here, we can say that theories and the researcher's background are prominent factors in qualitative research. This means that the researcher's own point of departure is combined with the participants' perspective, as the intention of qualitative research is to elicit the participant perspective. I will describe the researcher's different ways of seeing the research field below.

3.2 Inductive, Deductive and Abductive Approaches

When researchers try to understand and present the participant perspective they are following an "inductive approach". Knowing that a researcher always brings his or her subjective individual theory into the research, qualitative research can never be completely inductive. A qualitative researcher also realises that his or her research can never be objective, and that the research therefore always will have a value bias. The researcher should still strive to be aware of this subjectivity, but according to Heshusius (1994) it is difficult to notice your own subjectivity. One way of sharpening this awareness is to note down all the assumptions connected to the research you are planning to carry out. These assumptions will express which findings the researcher expects to find and are therefore an expression of the researcher's subjectivity. When qualitative researchers want to highlight the participant perspective they can make the participants' voices audible when presenting their research findings (Creswell, 2013). This shifting between theories and the researcher's perspective and the data material collected from the perspective of the participants is called an "abductive approach" (Alvesson & Sköldberg, 2009). The "deductive approach" is the opposite of the inductive approach. This means that the researcher and the theories that he or she brings into it direct the collection of material and the analysis of the data. The abductive approach is thus an approach in the interplay between the inductive and deductive approach.

4 Characteristics of the Qualitative Method

4.1 The Emic Perspective in Natural Settings

Qualitative research is a situated activity that localises the researcher in the real world. Qualitative researchers thus focus their research on natural settings and attempt to understand and interpret phenomena based on opinions ascribed to them by individuals in these settings (Denzin & Lincoln, 2011, p. 3). Interpretation, according to Ormiston and Schrift (1990), means that researchers uncover and express understanding. The qualitative researcher thus studies human or social processes in their natural setting; such studies are therefore also called naturalistic. In their studies, qualitative researchers endeavour to form a holistic or complex picture of participant perspectives within the research focus framing the study.

As mentioned above, the participant perspective is called the emic perspective. Wolcott (2008) describes the emic perspective as the counterpart of the etic perspective and discusses the origin of the concepts using the terms phonemic and phonetic. Phonemic represents the language forms in a specific language, while phonetic represents the meta-language and the general way any language can be described. In the research context Wolcott relates these concepts to the insider (emic) and outsider (etic) perspective: the emic perspective seeks to approach "the heart of what is under study, both literarily and figuratively" (p. 144). This means highlighting the understandings and opinions of the participants. Wolcott therefore cautions against adopting predefined categories which may conceal rather than describe the specifics in the processes studied in their real setting.

The qualitative researcher is also called a "bricoleur" who produces a "bricolage". The researcher assembles many pieces which together form a complex and holistic image of the research field and the people who are being studied (Denzin & Lincoln, 2011). The role of researchers in qualitative studies is also often compared to the role of a criminal investigator. Both attempt to find small pieces in a large puzzle which must be assembled before the case is solved or the picture is complete. They also have no choice but to accept uncertainty for an unspecified period of time (Merriam, 1998).

4.2 *The Purpose of Qualitative Research*

Sigrun Gudmundsdottir (2001) was deeply interested in classroom research, where the aim was to inspire and initiate discussion and debate so that the practice field could continue to develop and improve. A research text representing findings from the classroom should then be able to function as a thinking tool that could be of help in improving the teaching practice. I want to expand the aim of classroom research so that it also applies to research on all levels in school. If a research text is to be able to function as a thinking tool, the text basically has to invite the reader into the context and actions or phenomena that are being studied. It is then important for the researcher to write thick descriptions. Thick descriptions include both descriptions and the context of what is described, and the context functions as a framework of understanding. The difference between a blink of an eye as a blink and a blink of an eye as a hint is an example of respectively thin and thick descriptions. A thin description of the blink is to say that it is the rapid closing of the eyelid. A thick description will give this action a context which makes it possible to understand it (Geertz, 1973). Perhaps this blink is a romantic signal. Thick descriptions can help readers to recognise the situation and to adapt to and transfer findings in the text to their own setting and situation. The text then becomes a thinking tool (I will return to this concept in Chapter 9). There is no direct transfer of knowledge, but the descriptions in the text are adapted to their own situation. This is described as "naturalistic generalization" (Stake & Trumbull, 1982), which implies that the readers perceive what is read as parallel experiences adapted to their own situation. I will return to the importance of research-based knowledge in Chapter 8.

4.3 Ontology, Epistemology, Methodology and Axiology

Four different concepts represent content that both says something about qualitative research and about the researcher's role in such studies: "ontology", "epistemology", "methodology" and "axiology". According to Bateson (1972), all qualitative researchers are guided by general principles which combine views when it comes to these four concepts. They are called paradigms or fundamental sets of values that guide the action (Lincoln, Lynham, & Guba, 2011).

The concept of "ontology" refers to what exists and hence what we can know. What kind of beings are we and how can reality be described? The concept may thus be defined as the theory of being, i.e. the existence of things and their properties (Guba & Lincoln, 1989). The concept also has something to say about how reality will appear to a qualitative researcher (Creswell, 2013). As qualitative research lies within the constructivist paradigm, reality in qualitative research is created or constructed by the researcher and the people taking part in the study. The key ontological question thus refers to the conditions for calling something real. A qualitative researcher will answer that something is real if this reality is constructed by people in the current situation (Guba & Lincoln, 1988). According to Merriam (2002), the key to understanding qualitative research lies in the idea that meaning is socially constructed by individuals in their lifeworld, and this construction and understanding of reality is in continual change and development. Qualitative researchers are interested in understanding what these interpretations are at a specific point in time in a specific context. The researcher's goal is thus to attempt to understand and highlight the meaning people have constructed in relation to their lifeworld and their experiences (Merriam, 2002; Patton, 2002). In this way, attention is focused on the perspective of the participants, or the emic perspective, in qualitative studies. This perspective will, however, always be in interaction with the researcher's perspective, the etic perspective.

When it comes to Erik, he will be an insider and an outsider at the same time. He will attempt to commute between the outside and inside of the practice and culture he is part of when he is doing his research. Ry Nielsen and Repstad (2006) maintain that when the researcher is to analyse his or her organisation, the role that is assumed can be described as being both an ant and an eagle. Proximity and distance are then key concepts in this context. The role Erik has in his school means that in collaboration with the principal, Helene, he must understand the conditions as they are perceived by the school's teachers. This means that they must collect material to understand the current situation. They also intend to launch processes so that each teacher becomes aware of their own situation and practice in relation to the topic and field they want to have in focus so they can change and develop the practice. The common understanding of the current situation they eventually may develop will be the foundation on which to base the measures that they have decided to try together in school, and which Erik and Helene would like to study so they can understand how the process plays out and how important the measures will be. To create the necessary distance, Erik and Helene can read theory and write copiously in their logbook. This is what I did for my Master's thesis where I conducted research in my school (Postholm, Granum, & Gudmundsdottir, 1999). Theory is particularly important in research when the researcher is part of the community being studied. Because the researcher is on the home field, so to speak, "powerful glasses" are needed if he or she is to see anything in the research. Theories help to make the familiar alien so that it can be discovered and understood (Erickson, 1986). When a researcher notes down actions in the logbook, these actions are then separated from the original situation that is being recorded in the logbook (Ricoeur, 1981). The actions then take on a life of their own, which ensures that Erik and Helene can distance themselves from specific situations when they write about them in their logbook notes. Good qualitative research needs to be based on quality in the research and also quality in the knowledge provided by the research findings. The ethical principles must also be observed. This is particularly important when a researcher is examining his or her own organisation. I will discuss this in more detail in Chapter 8.

The concept of "epistemology" in qualitative research refers to the relationship between the researcher and the research participants (Guba & Lincoln, 1989). How can the relationship between the researcher and what is being studied be described? Instead of having objective distance, a close collaborative relationship is established in qualitative research between the researcher and the participants in settings that are the focus of the research (Guba & Lincoln, 1988). This is the role Helene and Erik will assume in the research at their own school. As the reality of the situation is constructed in the interaction between the researcher and the people in the study, some might think it superfluous to ask questions about this reality and what people already know. The dividing line between ontology and epistemology is therefore vague. Helene and Eric's school probably has a history which is important, for example, for understanding what the collaboration and relationships are like between the colleagues. The history and the cooperation relationships are not necessarily easy to grasp and understand, but I would claim that there is something within a reality that is easy to grasp and describe. This could be the number of classrooms and how these and the teachers' team rooms in the school are designed. There will be no disagreement about how many teachers have their work desks in each team room. How the collaboration between the teachers affects their teaching in the classroom may, however, lead to different points of view. The researcher can obtain an understanding of these points of view in the interaction with the participants. Thus the ontology and epistemology concepts may have their justification in qualitative research.

The concept of "methodology" refers to how we understand the world or acquire knowledge about it. Methodology is thus the theory of the approaches used in research and refers to the fundamental ways of acquiring knowledge. Examples of such methodological approaches are ethnographic studies and case studies. Methodology must not be confused with method, which refers to methods for collecting date and conducting an analysis. These methods are part of the methodology which also have a goal for the research and which moreover present a design for how this can be carried out. In Chapter 5 I will present six types of methodologies in qualitative research.

The term "axiology" refers to the theory of values. A common trait of all qualitative studies is that they have a value bias (Creswell, 2013). As described above, a qualitative researcher realises that the research is influenced by his or her subjective individual theory. This means that a qualitative study can never be value neutral. In qualitative studies it is therefore essential that the researcher, the most important instrument throughout the entire research process, presents his or her perspectives, assumptions and opinions to the reader, and discusses how these may have had impact on the analyses in and findings from the study. Presenting the researcher's point of view and influence will also help to assure the quality of the study in question. I will return to this in Chapter 8.

4.4   Research Questions in Research and DWR

Research questions in both qualitative research work and DWR often commence with "how" and "what". Occasionally the question *why* may also be used, but the intention then is not to find linear cause-effect relationships, but rather to describe the complexity of the research focus under study. When the researcher has found the aim of the research, it gives direction to how the research questions are formulated and which methodological approaches the researcher can choose to answer them. The aim of the research also helps the researcher to determine which informants or research participants should be invited to participate. Samples in such studies are therefore described as appropriate samples (Creswell, 2013). The interrogatives what, how and why, as presented above, give the research its direction which will then lead to a descriptive text. But it is still common that the researcher both analyses and discusses the findings that are brought to light. How a study can be presented in writing will be dealt with in Chapter 9.

4.5   Main Research Questions and Sub-Questions

As I have mentioned above, the substantive theories form the foundation on which concrete and researchable questions are formulated in qualitative research. Paradigms, theoretical models and intermediate theories will also help give direction to and framework for what the questions focus on. Even if the direction and framework of the research are clear, it is a challenge to formulate good research questions. The qualitative researcher wants to carry out the research in natural settings, and it will then be difficult to predict accurately in advance which data material the observations and interviews will yield. A researcher will strive to be as inductive in the research as possible, but will always bring personal, subjective, individual theories into the research, thus being abductive in the work (Alvesson & Sköldberg, 2009). The researcher can initially formulate a broad research question, which may eventually be narrowed down as the research process proceeds. A research question may basically be broad, but not so broad that everything and anything can be examined. It will have a focus but will not be too strictly focused because it must be open for new discoveries. Assumptions can also be formulated into sub questions which together can answer the main research question. In this way a researcher may also become aware of his or her subjectivity and test out his or her assumptions in the ongoing research. As a qualitative researcher willingly allows the research to bring new matters to light that he or she never considered, the research may lead to new research questions, and the researcher may then re-enter the research field with new assumptions during the course of the study. There will therefore always be interaction between theories which the researcher reads from and analyses in the data material to reach understanding throughout the entire research process. This switching between theory and the researcher and the data collected in the research field is presented in Figure 3.3.

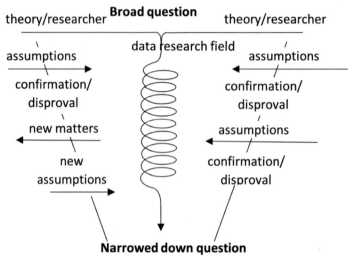

FIGURE 3.3   From broad to narrow research question

A broad main research question at the start of a research study could be: "How does the teacher collaboration help to promote the professional development of teachers in Valen school?" Research questions that may be asked in this context could be: "How is the teacher collaboration organised?", "Which aids do the teachers use in their collaboration?" and "How do teachers talk together when collaborating?" These sub-questions that I have made express our assumptions which build on our subjectivity and hence on theory we have also read. Perhaps the research process shows that the support the teachers have received from the teacher educator they have invited to the school as a supporting resource person in the teachers' professional development makes it necessary to narrow the main research question and to change the sub-questions. Or perhaps how the teachers talk together is not relevant in this study. Then, the sub-question could be replaced by: "How do the teachers experience the support they receive in their own learning processes?" The main research question can then be narrowed down as follows: "How does the support process help promote the teachers' professional development?"

4.6   *Development Questions*

If the issue to be studied is formed and narrowed down in DWR, a development question will also be formulated which frames and gives direction to the development work in the school. The professional development of teachers is defined as comprising the following elements: teachers' learning, how they learn to learn and how they use this knowledge in their practical activities (Avalos, 2011). The development question they agree at in the school could then be: "How do we need to collaborate to develop the relationship and communication with the pupils?" As I described in Chapter 1, it is essential that Erik and Helene spend time on developing topics and development questions that they will start with to improve practice. Pupils learn most and best when they can work with something they are interested in and motivated for, and this is exactly the same for teachers (Timperley, Wilson, Barrar, & Fung, 2007). In DWR work, how Erik and Helene lead and participate in the processes will then in all probability be very important. A traditional qualitative study also makes demands on the researcher, even if he or she is not supporting a development activity at the same time. I will present the challenges and opportunities for the researcher in both these roles below.

4.7 The Researcher's Challenges and Opportunities

A qualitative research project, whether it involves supporting development or not, presents researchers with a number of challenges and requirements. I will first present some general challenges and requirements which all qualitative researchers face, and then I will discuss what is required by a researcher in a DWR project. Challenges and opportunities connected with the researcher are that he or she:
- acquires knowledge about the topic to be studied in advance
- remains in the research field for so long a period of time that it is possible to present the complexity of the topic being studied
- endeavours to be aware of his or her own subjective individual theory which can influence the study and the findings presented
- is open to topics or matters that she or he had not thought about in advance that may surface during the research process
- is present in the research field during the entire data collection period
- has good communication skills and asks questions and listens to the research participants
- is able to collect data which may answer the main research question and sub-questions and is sensitive to the collected data
- is able to analyse large amounts of data
- realises that the researcher is the most important research tool in the entire research process
- writes descriptive detailed texts that express the complexity of the research field

– is interested in and wishes to write a detailed and descriptive text that expresses the participant perspective

When in addition to doing research the researcher has to also support the development processes he or she is studying, a number of competences will be needed. Based on their own work with close connection to schools, Postholm and Skrøvset (2013) have pointed out what can be required of a researcher who also functions as a supporting resource person for development:

- The researcher must have a high degree of self-respect, confidence in herself and the will to continue and not yield in the face of some opposition
- The researcher must be honest, not the least to herself, and emotionally receptive to impressions and expressions, thus functioning constructively in the exploratory partnership
- The researcher must allow the work to be process driven and must be prepared for unexpected events
- The researcher must accept surprises and listen with patience, and be open, creative and responsive
- The researcher gains authority, influence and trust through her competence
- The researcher has appreciative intelligence
- The researcher envisions positive development ahead, there is every probability that this is precisely what will happen. (p. 517)

These points can apply to researchers, whether or not they come from the outside and are working close up to a practice, and not least to Erik and Helene who assume this role in their own practice. In addition to the above, in their researcher roles I would add that Erik and Helene have the opportunity to use the data material that is collected and analysed on a continuous basis in the on-going development process. But this requires that they spend time on continuous analyses so that they can be related to the on-going development activities.

CHAPTER 4

Researcher Roles and Access to the Research Field

1   Introduction

In this chapter I will discuss the researcher role when researchers are to conduct research or carry out DWR, whether in their own school or other schools. I will first describe the researcher role where the researcher places herself or himself on the sidelines of the activity studied, and then I will examine the role the researcher has in DWR when interacting with the research participants. I will also discuss how a researcher can gain access to the research field or the people he or she wants to have as participants in the research.

2   Researcher Roles and the Aim of the Research

As mentioned above, the principal, Helene, and the teacher, Erik, want to conduct both research and DWR in their own school and to study other schools. The student teachers Leander and Leona also want to carry out research and conduct a limited DWR project. This means that they can have differing roles in the research activity. Prior to initiating the research, the researcher should decide which role he or she intends to adopt, and then stick to that role throughout the research project. It is an important ethical principle, in consideration of the research participants, to keep to the same role so they will be cognizant of the researcher's role and act accordingly. According to Glesne (2011), the role a researcher wants to assume depends on a number of conditions. It depends on the situation and aim of the research, and is also dependent on the researcher's theoretical stance and his or her personality and values. Below my main focus will be on the aim of the research and the researcher's background and point of departure.

A researcher may take on different roles in his or her own school and other schools. A student teacher who has not worked as a supply teacher in the school, and who does not want to study a school he or she is already familiar with will basically have a degree of distance to the settings and people to be studied. Teachers and leaders who conduct research in their own school, and thus in a familiar context, have a challenge in making the familiar alien so it can be analysed and understood. I will return to this later in the chapter. In the chapter on data collection (Chapter 6) I will describe different observer roles.

© KONINKLIJKE BRILL NV, LEIDEN, 2019 | DOI:10.1163/9789004410213_004

In this chapter I will look at the researcher's overarching role in the study, and therefore intend to deal with the researcher's role in the context of the aim of the research. I will examine the opportunities and challenges that arise when the research takes place in one's own school and therefore in a familiar context, and also in other contexts. First I will look at the researcher's role when the researcher defines herself or himself on the sidelines of the activity under study.

2.1   *The Researcher on the Sidelines*

When the student teacher, teacher and leader define their role as researcher on the sidelines of the activity being studied, the aim of the research may be to collect data material to develop understanding and knowledge that will end in a research text. This research may take place in the researcher's own school and in other schools. It is not an expressed goal in the research that the data collection and analysis of this material will be used in on-going development work. The text that is the result of this research can, however, still be used in connection with the coming DWR. The researcher might decide to conduct a narrative study to attempt to understand the motivation for development activities in a teacher team, or could decide to carry out an ethnographic study to determine whether there is collective responsibility in the school to promote the teachers' learning to improve the pupils' learning outcomes. The researcher could, on the other hand, focus on the school leaders and how teachers experience the support they give them in their learning process, or the researcher might study how the school leaders perceive their role as leaders of development activities. Phenomenological studies could be used to understand these perceptions. The researcher can also conduct a case study to examine how a time-limited teaching programme is carried out in a classroom.

These are all studies the researcher could carry out from the sidelines, examining the on-going activities without intervening in these activities, as well as conducting traditional interviews rather than using intervening focus-group interviews (see Chapter 6). Such a role and such studies will suit student teachers and teachers and leaders who do not want to carry out studies where the researcher's role is also supporting development processes while these are being studied. I will examine this in the next section "The interacting researcher".

2.2   *The Interacting Researcher*

In this section I will focus on the role of the researcher when it comprises supporting development processes while also undertaking research on these processes, i.e. when the researcher wants to carry out DWR and thus take part in the interaction with teachers and leaders. As I presented in Chapter 3, the research by Postholm and Skrøvset (2013) shows that when the researcher is supporting a development project while also doing research on it, he or she must have a high degree of self-respect and self-confidence, and the will to continue, not yielding in the face of small setbacks. In their research they also found that the researcher must be honest, also to herself/himself, and must be emotionally receptive to impressions and expressions, accepting them as input on how to relate to the research participants. Work in such a DWR project will be process driven, and their study shows that the researcher must expect the unexpected. This means that the researcher will not have complete control over the process and what happens but must expect surprises. A research finding in their study is also that the researcher gains authority, influence and trust through his or her competence. This means that the researcher must have competence that the research participants find relevant and useful for their development.

According to Engeström and Sannino (2010) the role of the researcher in DWR is to promote and maintain a development process which is led and owned by the practitioners (Engeström & Sannino, 2010, p. 15). This means that it is the leaders' and teachers' perceived need for change that should be the basis for formulating development questions relating to the object which teachers and leaders want to aim for. The researcher could collect mirror-data during the start-up phase (Cole & Engeström, 2007) so that the way the researchers, teachers and leaders understand the practice is discussed together to develop a common, deep and balanced understanding. This shared understanding describes the situation in the school which could then be the starting point for planning measures to move the practice towards a specific object. As mentioned in Chapter 2, Leont'ev (1981) has stated that "the object is the true motive" (p. 59). Teachers and leaders may find that the motivation lies in the object for the DWR if the work starts with challenges or opportunities they see in their practice. If ample time is spent on the start-up phase of development work so that everyone feels that the content is important for them, or at the least that they understand the aim of the work (Timperley, Wilson, Barrar, & Fung, 2007), then this phase can form the foundation and power centre for the future development of the work (Postholm, 2008a, 2018a).

Hammersley and Atkinson (2007) state that it is necessary to know a group's culture to be able to give credible explanations of the member's actions. Creswell (2013) and Glesne (2011) are more sceptical to research being performed within a known culture, and that it should take place in one's own institution. Glesne (2011) writes that it is easier for a researcher to study another culture than his or her own because it is easier to be open to new understandings when the setting is different to the one that you are normally in. Suppositions a researcher has will, according to Glesne, be challenged more in a setting that is new for the researcher. According to Glesne, roles could be confused when a teacher and principal also assume the researcher role because the other participants will be uncertain about which role they are assuming at different points in time.

The view held by Creswell (2013) and Glesne (2011) means that a researcher cannot be a full member of the group being researched. This does not apply when, for example, the teacher or leader is the one who is conducting DWR in their own school, according to Glesne (2011), because then the point is that everyone should learn together. I share the view that everybody should learn, but nevertheless believe that being a researcher in a school can be challenging. I would maintain that it is correct for the research if the researcher is aware of the challenges and acts accordingly. In Chapter 3 I referred to Ry Nielsen and Repstad's (2006) study of researchers about to conduct research in their own setting. They claim that the role assumed may be described as both being an ant and an eagle. This implies that the researcher has proximity to the research subject but should also attempt to make the known alien and also establish distance. In this context I described the logbook as a good tool for establishing distance, and I referred to Erickson (1986), who claims that theory can be a strategy which can help the researcher make the known alien so that distance is established. If, for example, Helene and Erik conduct studies in other schools while also carrying out DWR in their own school, the understanding they develop in the studies in the other schools will also shed light on the situation in their own school. Comparison between schools may thus help to broaden and develop the understanding of their own school and the activities there, while comparison will also help the researcher to establish some distance to what is familiar. Most likely we have all experienced obtaining a more nuanced perspective on what things are like at home when we are travelling. The saying "there's no place like home" also expresses this. We achieve distance to what is home and see it better when we are away.

The dual purpose of DWR must be mentioned before the work starts. In DWR it is important, as I have stated above, to be aware of the role and how "proximity" and "distance" to research may influence the researcher. These concepts may also be considered in relation to being an outsider and an insider and how different connections may influence the researcher in the work. Erik as the teacher and Helene as the principal will be insiders and have a proximity to the activity if their aim is to conduct DWR in their own school. Student teachers who want to carry out DWR in the school, and who have no connection to this school on a permanent basis, may define themselves as outsiders in the interaction, and thus will also have a distance to the activity. Below I will examine challenges and opportunities connected to the roles researchers can assume in

DWR. Before discussing the role of the student teachers as researchers in DWR, I will focus on the teachers and leaders in this role.

2.2.1 Leaders and Teachers in DWR

Experienced teachers and leaders have a different point of departure than a student teacher without experience from practice, but they might still feel that the role as a researcher and supporting resource person in the development work will both challenge them and provide opportunities if they are going to do research in their own school. When DWR is conducted in their own context, a researcher will in all probability be quite familiar with the field where the work is to take place. They know the culture (Hammersley & Atkinson, 2007). Because the researcher is also part of the context of the DWR, his or her gaze may also be veiled, and the researcher may feel that he or she is close to the on-going processes (Creswell, 2013). I have discussed above how the researcher can make the familiar alien. In DWR it is not only a matter of the researcher, in this case the teacher and leader, having to assume the researcher role. He or she must also be acknowledged in this role by the others in the school to have legitimacy for intervening in the practices of the others, which is done by offering ideas and asking questions (see questions in interviews and intervening focus-group interviews, Chapter 6). For the researcher, it is not only about having the relevant competence, but also about developing relationships with colleagues in school so they trust the researcher and believe that he or she is genuinely motivated to ensure that everybody learns, as Glesne (2011) states, and that they therefore have confidence in the teacher or leader in all roles, as colleagues and as supporting resource persons and researchers in DWR.

If leaders and teachers want to assume the researcher role in DWR in another school, they may be able to avoid switching between the role of teacher and the role of researcher in their collaboration with other teachers and leaders. In another school they may be seen as researchers if they make it clear what their role is when interacting with teachers and leaders. They will also be outsiders and have distance to the processes they are to support and research.

2.3 The Student Teacher in DWR

When student teachers are to support and conduct research on a development project, they can face a number of challenges and opportunities. Student teachers may have competence that is experienced as useful for others, but they may feel that supporting experienced teachers and leaders in school is a major challenge, even when they have relevant knowledge to offer. In such a situation the student teacher can study schools and the practice in them by understanding how the practice has been and how it is now (see the expansive learning cycle in Chapter 2) as a stage in DWR without the student teacher being used as a supporting resource person in development processess. The text this research will lead to may be a good tool in the further DWR in the school.

If the student teacher is to avoid feeling alone with experienced leaders and teachers in the school, he or she may also enter into collaboration with a teacher who would like to test a teaching programme with the student. Another possibility is that the student teacher conducts DWR with his or her supervisor in the school and in this way does not work with experienced leaders and teachers alone. Assuming the researcher role together with one's supervisor or a group of teacher educators/researchers in DWR can also create a learning community around supporting development activities and show how to research this. As a participant in this learning community, the student teacher will participate in interviews and observations and gain insight into how experienced teacher educators/researchers conduct interviews, how they act in the observer role, how they deal with research participants and how they analyse the collected material. This suggests that a student teacher should have the opportunity to participate in a learning community composed by a group of teacher educators.

2.4 *The R&D Model and the Researcher Role in DWR*

The R&D model (Postholm & Moen, 2011) presented in Chapter 2 may be useful for everyone, the student teacher, teacher educators/researchers, leaders and teachers, whether in their own or other schools, if they are to carry out DWR. This model shows the development process, how the researchers and research participants can have a meta-view on the development processes and how the researcher can direct the focus on the research questions or his or her researcher gaze on all the data material that has been collected to answer the research questions. The researcher can move between these three levels (the primary circle, the secondary circle and the researcher plateau) during the entire research process, and the model may help the researcher to be aware of which role he or she has in the different phases or points in time in the DWR. The model also shows that the researcher can basically switch between these roles at the same time. This means that the researcher may include data material, an analysis of it and provide preliminary research findings during the development work so that the research supports this activity while it is still going on. The data material that the researchers collect during the research process in DWR is, as we have seen, called "mirror data" (Cole & Engeström, 2007). As the name suggests, the data material may reflect back to the teachers and leaders how the studied processes play out, thus becoming a tool for conversations in further development work.

3   Access to the Research Field

When the researcher has decided which role to assume and therefore also the aim of the research, the next stage is to contact the schools if the intention is to carry out the research or DWR in other schools than his or her own. Then access is needed to the research field and the consent of the chosen participants must be obtained. In all cases, whether the research or DWR is to take place in one's own school or not, research participation must be formalised: the participants must give their written consent. Below I will examine how the researcher can proceed both when coming to a school and when working in the school where the research or DWR is to be conducted.

3.1   *Research on the Sidelines in One's Own Context or Others' Context*

When a researcher conducts research outside his or her own school or educational institution, whether this is inexperienced student teachers or experienced teachers or leaders in a Master's degree programme, the researcher must first determine which school to conduct the research in. The choice of school will depend on the aim of the research. If the researcher wants to understand and describe a good school practice, one school might be chosen for the study because it is known for having a good cooperative teaching environment where the pupils have high achievement rates. The researcher may then carry out an "internal case study" (Stake, 1995, see Chapter 5). If the researcher wants to describe a good practice, whether outside or inside a school classroom, the point is to find a school which can contribute precisely that. Educational institutions collaborate with schools and may therefore maintain an overview of practices in different schools. The student teacher may therefore ask the supervisor which school would be appropriate to choose, or he or she may have acquaintances that can suggest where the study could be carried out. Experienced leaders and teachers studying at a teaching college have in all probability collaborated with other schools and leaders and teachers that can help them to choose a school based on the aim of the research.

As mentioned above, before the research is started, it benefits all the parties if the researcher has defined his or her own role, and a declaration of consent form has been sent to the participants in the school in question. Usually the principal is the gatekeeper, but the researcher is recommended to ask the teachers and leaders in question first (Bogdan & Biklen, 2007; Glesne, 2011) as it may be difficult for the principal to consent to research if she or he does not know whether the potential participants, leaders and teachers actually want to participate. If the researcher does not know of teachers and leaders who can be asked in advance, one solution can be to ask the principal for his or her ideas about potential participants. In such a situation the researcher should present criteria for the preferred participants. This could be, perhaps, that they work on a particular team, that they teach specific subjects, that they have little or a high degree of experience and that they have a varied educational background. Another criterion might refer to the whole school, for example that leaders and teachers have worked on a joint development activity over time. An example of a letter sent to schools that had participated in *Ungdomstrinn i utvikling* [Lower secondary school in development], a national programme in 2013–2017, is presented in Appendix 1. In consultation with the principal after it had determined that the school would like to participate in this research programme, more specific criteria were presented relating to which type of teachers and pupils were preferred in the study.

Bogdan and Biklen (2007) have described five points a researcher should consider before starting the research. I believe that these five relevant points should also be included in an invitation letter to participate in the research project, and the researcher should have them in mind when conducting research on the sidelines in one's own and other schools. They are:

1. *What are you actually going to do?*
   According to the two authors, the researcher should give a precise explanation about the aim of the research and how the researcher intends to come to an understanding of the topic he or she wants to research. Here the research questions should be presented along with an explanation of how the data is to be collected.

2. *Will you be disruptive?*
   The leaders and teachers will be concerned about whether the researcher is intending to intervene in or disrupt their work procedures. According to the authors, it is important to assuage any concerns and tell the participants that the researcher does not intend to take up too much of their time, and will be sensitive to their problems and needs.

3. *What are you going to do with your findings?*
   Many people ask this question because they fear negative publicity or the political use of the information the researcher collects. The researcher should therefore explain very clearly what the point of the research is. It is important here to tell the participants who the research text is intended for and that all names will be made anonymous.

4. *Why us?*

   Here researchers can tell the potential participants that they have heard about the school and the practice there, and that this information led them to want to know more. Another reason can be that the school and the people the researcher wants to participate in the project can help to illuminate a particular topic that he or she wants to study.

5. *What will we get out of it?*

   Leaders and teachers in schools that participate in research should be allowed to expect something in return from the project when they agree to participate. The researcher should therefore decide what can be offered. Some schools want feedback on what the researcher has discovered. They may want the end report or they may want the researcher to come to the school to talk about the findings after project completion. The authors warn that researchers should not try to promise too much and add that promises must be kept. (pp. 87–88)

When the researcher is invited or offers to go to the school to conduct DWR the start-up phase is somewhat different. However, in the role the researcher adopts he or she will reflect on how this work should be explained to the participants.

3.2   *Research in the Interaction in One's Own and Other's Contexts*

In DWR the start-up phase is somewhat different than in research conducted on the sidelines. The researcher may want the whole school, all its leaders and teachers, to participate in the DWR, or it could be a teacher or leader team or one teacher in his or her own teaching practice. Perhaps the whole school, a team or a teacher want to participate. How a DWR project is initiated will in all probability influence the further work. The research questions raised in a DWR project may be the researcher's, they may stem from teachers and leaders, or the researchers and teachers and leaders in a school may develop a research or a development question for the DWR project together (Postholm & Madsen, 2006). Whether the researcher is invited or invites him or herself into a DWR project in a school, the collaboration should be formalised. This means that in both cases the researcher must write a letter containing the points made by Bogdan and Biklen (2007). In this project the researcher will also be conducting research, and teachers and leaders should be informed in the same way as when the researcher is on the sidelines in other contexts, both when it comes to the researcher role and how the findings will be published and used.

It will be relevant to submit information under point 1, as well as point 2 which refers to how the researcher will proceed in the development work and in the research. Point 3 will also be relevant, while point 4 will be addressed if the researcher has invited him- or herself to the school. Point 5 deals with what teachers and leaders or possibly the whole school will gain from participating in the project. In DWR the intention is that the participants should receive support in their own development processes, thus benefiting from participation while the DWR is on-going. Moreover, the findings and the text the research leads to could also be used in the further development work as a development tool. Thus research participants will profit doubly from their participation, but this means that the researcher has to return something (point 5) after the project has come to its end. The teachers and leaders may receive the published Master's thesis, the researcher may present the findings, or, what is best if the DWR project has functioned well, the researcher may continue in his or her role in the school and use the findings as the basis and tool in further DWR.

When the DWR project is carried out in one's own school, the researcher should also clarify with the others in the school how the research should be conducted (point 1) and the role he or she will play in the development processes (point 2). How the findings from the research will be published should also be presented to the colleagues (point 3), and also why the researcher wants to carry out this work in his or her school (point 4). In the start-up phase the researcher may explain that he or she intends to support development processes, which means that the colleagues will gain something, and that he or she will present the findings after the project so that these may form the point of departure for pauses for reflection leading to knowledge on which to base further development in the school (point 5).

CHAPTER 5

Qualitative Research Approaches and Analysis

1   Introduction

There is a close relationship between the researcher and participants in all qualitative studies, and, as stated in Chapter 3, the research approaches can therefore be defined within the constructivist paradigm. This also applies if a text is the focus of the study. Understanding is constructed in the interaction between the voices the text represents and the reader/researcher. The epistemological stance is thus that knowledge is created in the interaction between the researcher and the field under study (Guba & Lincoln, 1989). Below I will present four qualitative methodologies or approaches: case studies, ethnographic studies, phenomenological studies and narrative studies. I will examine each of these approaches under the headings "Characteristic features and goals", "data collection" and "analysis". I will present an analytical method for each approach, even if the constant comparative analysis method presented in Chapter 7 can be used in all the approaches (Strauss & Corbin, 1990, 1998; Corbin & Strauss, 2008). I will also present text analysis and conversation analysis as separate analytical methods in this chapter, which explains why "analysis" is included in the title. These methods of analysis can be part of their own studies, or they can be embedded in studies that are framed by the methodologies mentioned above. I do not present D-analysis (Middleton, 2010) here, because this analysing method is used within the frame of CHAT and DWR, and thus not used it its own study as a methodology. I present D-analysis together with the constant comparative analysis method in Chapter 7, using a study as an example to show how these two methods can be combined.

As all the approaches presented here are qualitative they may overlap. However, I still recommend that the researcher should choose to use one approach and then use it thoroughly. The aim of the research will determine which methodology or approach the researcher chooses and will also determine which questions the researcher asks. When the aim is clear and the questions have been formulated, the researcher is ready to choose the approach. The aim of the research will also determine the sample selected for the research, and is therefore called an appropriate sample (Postholm, 2010).

2 Case Studies

2.1 *Characteristic Features and Goals*

The aim of a case study is to present thorough understandings of a single case or to explore a case or problem area by studying several cases to illustrate the matter or problem thoroughly (Creswell, 2013). As case studies are limited to time and place, they are described as bounded systems (Creswell, 2013; Stake, 1995). Case studies can focus on an individual, several individuals, a group, a complete programme, an activity, an organisation or a partnership. However, it may be difficult to determine the limitations on time, place, actions and processes in a case study. If the study does not have a clear starting point and a clear end, the researcher will have to decide its scope (Creswell, 2013).

Researchers disagree whether case studies should be considered as a methodology or as "something" to be studied. Stake (1995) maintains that researchers make their selection precisely because they want to focus on one case or a number of cases. He therefore does not consider case studies as a methodology, while others present case studies as a research strategy or methodology (Creswell, 2013; Merriam, 1998).

The "case" that is studied using the case study as the methodology could be, for example, a school-based competence development project in one or more schools. If the aim is to highlight findings from a particular school because it is exemplary and unique, the researcher will choose to conduct an "internal case study". If, on the other hand, the researcher wants to illuminate a case, such as school-based competence development, a single case or several cases may be chosen to illustrate precisely this point. If the researcher chooses one case, this will be an "instrumental case study". When several cases are chosen to illuminate a particular point this is a "collective case study". When conducting instrumental case studies and collective case studies, the aim is then not to describe a single case, but to illuminate a case or a problem area (Stake, 1995).

When the data material in a case study has been collected, the researcher presents thorough descriptions of the case or cases in context. The topic or specific situations which have been identified and analysed will also be presented. The presentation of the study of a case or cases will therefore include a description structured according to the topic the researcher has deduced during the study. The topics developed in a case or cases may be presented as a theoretical model (Creswell, 2013). Case studies usually end with the researcher's conclusions based on the total findings from the study (Stake, 1995), or by summing up what can be learnt from the study (Creswell, 2013). In case studies, the researcher has rich data material that serves as the basis for the analyses and the findings that are summarised from them.

2.2 Data Collection

A researcher will use many data collection strategies when gathering information in case studies: interviews, observations, studies of documents and audio-visual material, and examination of physical artefacts (objects) (Creswell, 2013). Using information collected from many sources may help the researcher to develop an understanding and to present the case or cases thoroughly in context.

2.3 Analysis of Case Studies

The point of case-study analysis is to contribute to detailed descriptions of the case and its context. The aim of the analysis is, moreover, to find meaning in the data and to develop understanding of the case being studied (Stake, 1995). According to Stake (1995), the researcher has both a specific and a general interest. What is important is to understand individual situations or actions, and to understand the case so that the research on this case can have relevance for other similar cases. Stake (1995) claims that the process of analysis is characterised by creativity and intuitive processes that generate meaning and understanding, and that the study itself, the focus of the research question and the researcher's curiosity determine which analytical strategy is to be used. He mentions two strategies for carrying out this process: direct analysis and categorical aggregation. Below I will describe these two approaches.

2.3.1 Direct Analysis

Direct analysis means that the researcher analyses individual events. The researcher sees no need to look for confirmation from additional incidents, events or situations, but builds his or her understanding on a single situation. Stake (1995) describes a situation in the classroom where he as the researcher was unable to understand everything the teacher said to the pupils when he observed the classroom the first time. He was not interested in searching for what he calls aggregating instances or events which might reinforce his perception of the situation. He did not understand everything the teacher told the pupils or did with them in his teaching, but the teacher was obviously pleased with his understanding of the situation. Stake saw that the pupils found the situation comprehensible and therefore he called it "the teacher's understanding of the classroom". Stake writes that he could have learnt much about how dialects and cultural backgrounds influenced the situation, but he gave meaning to the data material collected in one setting without feeling the need for more data that could confirm his analysis. He focused on one pupil. This pupil behaved in such a way that he had expected other reactions from the teacher than what actually occurred. The teacher obviously stretched the rules when it came to this boy. Stake observed several situations where the boy acted in such a way that he expected the teacher to intervene and stop him, for example when he pushed a broom into the feet of another pupil. He wondered why the teacher tackled the situation the way he did, but he did not abandon his analysis of the situation, and his focus remained on the pupil. He did not question how consistent the pupil was in his interaction with other pupils, how often this happened, whether he would do it in the presence of others, what some of the correlates of this behaviour could be and how common this behaviour was among boys in Year 6. He was intent to keep his focus on the boy. In the direct analysis the researcher asks: What is this a case of? What does it mean? (Stake, 1995). When working on other topic areas in the school, Stake (1995) had to focus on several conditions to be able to understand them. Then he would need to gather material that could contribute to categorical aggregation.

2.3.2   Categorical Aggregation

Categorical aggregation refers to finding patterns. Sometimes these are known in advance, while other times they emerge in the analysis (Stake, 1995). Categorical aggregation means that information is collected in different settings and situations to understand, for example, the professionality of teachers. This then means reaching an understanding according to a repetition of events. Some incidents may confirm earlier understandings, while others may disprove them. When a process plays out like this, patterns or categories emerge in the course of the study. This shows how the researcher from the very first moment in the field commences the process of analysing to understand. Categorical aggregation may be carried out within a case and for several cases. Yin (2009) calls analysis with a focus on two or more cases a cross-case analysis.

2.3.3   Naturalistic Generalisation

Stake (1995) clearly admits that his analyses and interpretations are subjective. Therefore, what he is attempting to do is to write descriptions that help readers make their own analyses and interpretations. For this reason they must be thick descriptions (Geertz, 1973), where the readers experience that what they are reading is a parallel or vicarious experience. This means that the readers find the descriptions of situations and settings similar to what they have personally experienced, and then adapt them to their situation. Stake and Trumbull (1982) call this naturalistic generalisation. I will examine this form of generalisation in Chapter 8. Stake (1995) points out that it is important that the researcher explains the basis for his or her own analyses and interpretations in the text to support the reader's naturalistic generalisations.

3   Ethnographic Studies

3.1   *Characteristic Features and Goals*

While ethnographic studies originated in anthropological studies they are more restricted in their scope. Anthropologists, and particularly British ones, carried out comparative studies to make generalisations based on people's social lives. They have traditionally referred to these generalisations as "cultural universals" (Wolcott, 2008, p. 248). The first ethnographic studies focused on "the others" in primitive cultures, while "the others" now studied by ethnographers resemble the researchers themselves and the culture they are in. The ideal unit for an ethnographic study is, according to Wolcott (2008), the study of one aspect of something to reach the core of what is being studied. In ethnographic studies the researcher therefore often focuses on one social group (Wolcott, 2008). This group may be the whole teaching staff in a school, it may be a teacher team, a teacher in this school, or the school leaders.

Erik, the teacher, and Leander, the student teacher, can use this approach if, for example, they want to understand the actions and opinions of the teachers in a team. The research question may then be: "How do the teachers collaborate?" If Erik wants to study the leadership in his school or another school he may then ask: "How do the leaders arrive at decisions?" The intention is to understand the culture in the teacher team and among the leaders. Questions asked in ethnographic studies often start with "what" to produce a descriptive text, but underlying questions must also be asked to understand meaning ascribed to actions and to give a comprehensive description.

Culture refers to the different ways that groups act and which convictions they relate to these actions. The researcher does not study the culture but rather the ordinary social behaviour of people. The culture does not exist before the researcher has described how the people being studied have carried out actions and what they think about them. The concept of culture must therefore be introduced by the researcher, as it does not spontaneously stand out in the data material. The concept of culture is abstract and a perspective for studying human processes with particular focus on acquired social behaviour. The researcher thus assumes responsibility for making the culture explicit in everything he or she observes and hears (Wolcott, 2008).

An ethnographic study ends with a cultural portrait (Creswell, 2013), or a holistic picture of how the people studied live and act (Fetterman, 2010). "Ethno" refers to people and "graph" to image, which then means drawing an image of the people being studied. This means that ethnography is not the study of a culture but rather the study of the social actions that are identifiable for the group or individual under study. Ethnographers study specific people in specific settings, meaning that this approach is the study of the specific, and as described here they will always be studies of a micro-culture (Wolcott, 2008). What characterises ethnographic studies is that the researcher must remain in the setting for a long enough time to be able to develop an understanding that can lead to a written cultural portrait. The researcher therefore does not know in advance how long he or she will be in the research field (Postholm, 2010). Bearing in mind that the researcher stays in the field for extended periods of time in ethnographic studies, there is always the danger of the researcher "going native", which will make it difficult to see and analyse. The researcher's view may be undermined where he or she becomes like "the fish in the water" (Kluckhohn, 1949). This can be a major challenge when carrying out research in one's own school. How a researcher can proceed in such a case is described in Chapter 4.

A key feature of ethnographic studies is that the context for the actions must be described, "lots of it", according to Wolcott (2008, p. 84), and the descriptions must include relevant and complex details. Ethnographic studies thus provide "thick descriptions", which means that actions are described in their context so they can be understood (Geertz, 1973). This then means that there is a strong descriptive element in ethnographic studies, and the voices of the participants are elicited through extracted quotations that are part of the description. The emic perspective is thus prominent in ethnographic studies, as in all qualitative studies (Creswell, 2013). Even if the term culture is not defined or used in the presentation of the study, the reader must be able to assess in which ways the underlying perception of culture has guided the researcher in the study, which is the main goal of ethnographic studies.

3.2   *Data Collection*

Fieldwork is the foundation of ethnographic studies. Wolcott (2008) presents three main forms of data collection in such studies: participatory observations, interviews and analysis of documents. He also describes these methods using the terms: "experience", "inquiry" and "review". He relates "experience" to participatory observation where the researcher gains first-hand experience of occurring events through both seeing and hearing. Wolcott points out that the observations are also the researchers' personal experiences so that they should not strive for the principle of objectivity, but rather endeavour to be aware of and highlight their subjectivity. In Chapter 6 I will elaborate on how observations can be carried out, but it is sufficient to mention here what Wolcott (2008) claims. He describes observation as following the natural activity and communication in a group and also describes the observer as the shadow. "Inquiry" may initially be perceived as being part of participatory observation, but according to Wolcott (2008), the researcher is far more active when he or she starts to ask questions about what is occurring. Asking questions, according to him, is something completely different, as the researcher intervenes in or initiates activities and communication between the people he or she is studying or between the researcher and the research participant. "Review" means that the researcher examines what has already been produced by others. This could be documents accessible to everyone in an archive, or more personal writings, such as letters, diaries and pictures. Art objects, recordings of music or speech, various objects or anything that can be shared with the ethnographer and not necessarily others can be reviewed. In addition to observation and interviews, Fetterman (2010) also uses the concepts symbols and artefacts about sources that may give the researcher information for understanding actions and opinions related to them. In the school, it may be interesting for Helene and Erik to study which objects the teachers have in their classrooms or workrooms and then ask them what they think about the placement of these objects.

3.3   *Analysis*

The overarching intention and direction of ethnographers is to conduct cultural analyses and interpretations. The established patterns that are developed from repeated actions collectively constitute the abstraction and the concept of culture. The result of a specific ethnographic study is a collation of the personality and biography of the ethnographer in interaction with a specific location in a unique way. The understanding which is developed in an ethnographic study therefore becomes a social construction of reality, and the researcher acknowledges that he or she has impact on the analysis and interpretation (Wolcott, 2008). In this construction the emic and the etic perspectives are united (Creswell, 2013). The people ethnographers interact with in the field, such as teachers and leaders in schools, are considered research participants or cooperation partners, and not subjects or informants (Wolcott, 2008). This approach to concepts can apply to all qualitative studies as they are carried out within a constructivist paradigm.

When describing different phases in the research activity, Wolcott (1994) distinguishes between description, analysis and interpretation. Description is the bedrock or foundation of the narrative. The analysis presents facts, figures and findings. Leading up to this presentation the researcher has studied the material to find patterns. Is there something that is repeated and which can be seen in context? The patterns the researcher identifies can state something about what people say, what they do and which expectations they have in connection with actions they initiate themselves. The data material can then be sorted into categories developed according to the patterns the researcher sees in the material. When the researcher proceeds in this way in the analysis, the constant comparative analysis method can be used. This analysis method is presented in Chapter 7.

The interpretation is focused on what the researcher understands from the analysis. What does the analysis mean? Which implications does the analysis have? This is comparable to how we understand a picture. If we are examining a picture and trying to determine which techniques the painter has used, and looking at which colours the painter has mixed, we are analysing within the frame of the picture. This can be compared to facts and findings derived from the data material. When we try to understand the painter's message, we leave the frame and may for example attempt to understand and interpret the motif common to the epoch it was painted in. What does the painter want to tell us? What is the painter's message? (Postholm, 2010). This is an interpretation which can be compared to what an ethnographer does when writing about the implications of the findings in a study.

The researcher makes the collected material comprehensible using terms from his or her own cultural framework (Wolcott, 2008). Eisner (1997) maintains that artists do not paint what they see, but that they see what they know they can paint. Wolcott (2008) has adapted this idea to ethnography, stating that ethnographers do not describe what they see, but that they see what they are able to describe. In the end the ethnographer ends up with a holistic narrative about the culture, one which contains description, analysis and interpretation. The narrative is "an overall picture of how a system works" (Fetterman, 2010, p. 10), and this narrative may start with a teacher, a leader, a team or a school as an organisation.

4   Phenomenological Studies

4.1   *Characteristic Features and Goals*

Phenomenological studies describe the shared meanings individuals have about life experiences (Creswell, 2013). This type of study can have several forms. My point of departure is hermeneutic (interpretative) phenomenology (van Manen, 1990, 2016) and descriptive psychological phenomenology (Giorgi, 1985; Moustakas, 1994). Giorgi and Moustakas write that phenomenological studies describe the meaning people ascribe to a perception connected to experiencing a phenomenon. Van Manen (2016) states that phenomenological studies aim to understand the identity or essence of a phenomenon or event. Hermeneutic phenomenology is not just descriptive because the researcher also interprets the meanings relating to the life experiences. "The researcher 'mediates' between the different meanings" (Van Manen, 1990, p. 26). In psychological phenomenology, the goal is also to arrive at the essence of the phenomenon being studied (Giorgi, 1985; Moustakas, 1994). Essence is not understood as universal essence (Husserl, 1983), but an essence that depends on the context or lifeworld the research participants are in. The findings are general in the sense that the descriptions are related to the phenomenon, thus moving away from the concrete situations where the material was collected. Giorgi (1985) reminds us that the relationship between the experiences of the research participants is what constitutes this essence, and that it must be understood according to the contextual factors. Generalisation can therefore take place between similar contextual situations.

The intention of phenomenological studies is to understand everything that can be experienced in the consciousness of people in their lifeworld. "Lifeworld" refers to our day-to-day reality which we live and act in. What is experienced can be an object, a person or a complex situation (Giorgi, 1985), such as learning or development in school-based competence development. Research questions could relate to how teachers experience the contribution of teacher educators to development in the school, how they experience the way leaders take charge of this work and how they experience the tensions between new and old practice. The research focus could also be on learning and how learning is experienced on different levels in school. As in all qualitative studies, the idea is to understand through the perspective of the conscious experience of the person in the study. The researcher conducts accurate analyses of how the phenomenon or event is experienced by the person who is experiencing it (Giorgi, 1985). The researcher attempts to suspend judgment (epoché) or bracket his or her own assumptions and prejudices relating to the phenomenon being studied so he or she can enter the research in as unbiased a way as possible (Giorgi, 1985; Moustakas, 1994; Van Manen, 2016). As I have already dealt with in Chapter 3, it is difficult to be aware of one's own subjectivity (Heshusius, 1994), but this is still something a researcher must strive for. The researcher must try to be aware of his or her subjectivity and present this as part of the context of the findings. As we shall see, the researcher's personal relationship to a phenomenon is part of the analytical procedure that Moustakas (1994) has developed.

In psychological phenomenology the essence is not interpreted but is rather described precisely in a descriptive analysis. However, not everything will be described. Giorgi (1985) describes this as a figure-background relation, stating that all elements in an experience cannot be described. Interpretation in phenomenology means introducing something not directly connected to the phenomenon or event that has been experienced. This may be a theory to illuminate the findings, or hypotheses or assumptions deduced from the findings (Giorgi, 1985; Van Manen, 2016). This is the intention in hermeneutic phenomenology (van Manen, 1990, 2016). In psychological phenomenology, the researcher presents a second-order description of the research participants' description, where concepts within the psychological tradition are used to label the experiences of the participants. Giorgi (1985) maintains that psychological phenomenology can also be adapted to other disciplines, such as pedagogy where pedagogical concepts, such as the experiential concept, the zone of proximal development and professionality, can be related to the data material (see intermediate theories and concepts in Chapter 3). In this work, according to Giorgi (1985), the researcher adopts an intersubjective attitude to the collected material, helping us to hear its echo in the constructivist position within the context of knowledge development.

4.2   Data Collection

The researcher usually collects data for these studies through transcribed interviews but can also observe situations and use documents as data sources (Giorgi, 1985). In hermeneutic phenomenology a researcher will often use observations, as the body is also considered a source for understanding how the phenomenon or event has been experienced (Van Manen, 2016). The researcher describes experiences relating to the phenomena or events he or she is interested in. The participants must have experienced the phenomenon or event that the researcher would like to describe and understand. They might be asked to write a description of their experience, but people do not commonly write as exhaustively as they speak (Giorgi, 1985). To get a full grasp of experiences, research participants usually contribute retrospective descriptions of their own experiences and meanings relating to them (Giorgi, 1985).

Such studies normally have three to ten (Dukes, 1984) or five to 25 participants (Polkinghorne, 1989). According to Creswell (2013) a heterogeneous group should be used. If the essence described is to have significance for similar contextual situations, however, this demands that an essence across the research participants can be described. If three persons are participating in the study, I would recommend that they have been selected according to the same criteria and that they have experience from the same context. How pupils who have poor learning outcome in a primary school experience their learning situation will most probably be different from how high-performing pupils at another lower secondary school experience their situation.

The phenomenologist wants to arrive at answers to the questions "what" and "how", what is experienced in the consciousness and how or under which conditions, and in which context the phenomenon or event has been experienced

(Giorgi, 1985; Moustakas, 1994). The researcher must therefore ask both the what and the how questions in the interview with the participants. The material obtained using these questions forms the first-order description, the direct description of the experience of the participants, which the researcher then uses to present a second-order description. I will return to these descriptions below.

4.3 Phenomenological Analysis

Giorgi (1985) presents the phenomenological analysis as a three-stage process:
1. Reading to gain an understanding of the whole
2. Developing units of meaning
3. Transforming the statements made by the participants into psychological-phenomenological expressions

The first stage (1) means reading the entire transcript to gain an impression of the whole. According to Giorgi (1985), the phenomenological approach is holistic, as the view is that meaning can be deduced from the entire transcription, from beginning to end. The next stage (2) is to develop units of meaning, as it is impossible to present the transcription in its entirety. Giorgi maintains that the units of meaning must be sensitive to the psychological-phenomenological perspective. When it comes to research in school, educational theories may, as mentioned, be the point of departure for the researcher, and the meaning units that are developed are therefore sensitive to such theories and concepts. Giorgi describes the third stage (3) as the core of the analytical method. The researcher now deals with the material which has been categorised into meaning units to present a second-order description. The units of meaning constitute the structure or the second-order descriptions and are related to theory. The theory is not applied to interpret the material, but to put the findings into words and abstract them, according to Giorgi's context, into the psychological discipline (Giorgi, 1985, pp. 128–137).

Moustakas (1994) presents additional analytical methods, and I find his modification of the approach, called the Stevick-Colaizzi-Keen method, both practical and useful, and therefore worth describing here. The procedure is:
1. The researcher first tries to achieve an understanding of his experience of the phenomenon being studied.
2. From the verbatim transcriptions the researcher takes the following steps:
    a. Considers each statement with respect to its significance for the description of the phenomenon.
    b. Records all relevant statements.
    c. Lists each non-repetitive and non-overlapping statement. These constitute the meaning units of the experience.
    d. Relates and clusters the meaning units under themes.

  e. Synthesises the meaning units and themes into a textural description for each participant. Includes verbatim examples (this description includes what has been experienced in its context (how)).
  f. Reflects on the textural descriptions and describes the structure of the experience for each participant (connects the description to concepts with the theoretical perspective).
  g. Constructs a joint textural-structural description of the meanings and the essences of the experience. This description presents the essence of experiences relating to the phenomenon (p 122, cited with some modifications and explanations).

Hermeneutic phenomenology presents a thematic analysis, but Van Manen (2016) points out that analysing life experiences is a complex and creative process, and that developing and formulating a thematic understanding is not a rule-bound process. To illuminate the theme and insight, the researcher can use three different approaches, according to Van Manen:

1. A holistic reading approach: The researcher reads the entire text and creates a sentence that covers the meaning content.
2. A selective reading approach: The researcher reads the text several times to discover which statements are essential or which express the phenomenon or experience that is being described. These can form the basis for developing and writing the text.
3. A detailed reading approach: The researcher focuses his attention on every single sentence or sentence cluster and asks what this sentence or sentence cluster expresses about the phenomenon or experience that is being described. The researcher tries to identify the thematic expressions, statements or narrative paragraphs that show the meanings relating to the experience. (Van Manen, 2016, p. 320)

A phenomenon or an experience can thus (a) be described by a research participant, recorded and transcribed, (b) be rewritten into an anecdote (c) be processed by holistic, selective or line by line thematisations, which (d) become the point of departure for the researcher's writing.

5 Narrative Studies

5.1 *Characteristic Features and Goals*

The "narrative" in narrative studies can be both the phenomenon and the method (Clandinin & Connolly, 2000). This means that the researcher either studies narratives told by teachers in Valen school, for example, about how they experience their collaboration in school, or that it is the method the researcher uses in the research when constructing narratives based on what has been told. Czarniawska (2004) defines a narrative approach as a spoken or written text which gives a description of an event/action in chronological order (p. 17). The researcher will often study one or two persons, will collect data by listening to their stories and then will present them by highlighting the meanings connected to the experiences, often represented by life phases (Creswell, 2013). "Narrative research refers to stories lived and told", Clandinin and Connolly have claimed (2000, p. 20). For the researcher to be able to reproduce their stories, active collaboration with the research participants is required, and the researcher also has to be aware of his or her own background and how this can have impact on the research process (Creswell, 2013).

Narrative studies can have many forms. Researchers can collect stories from people, individually and in groups, as well as from documents. They can sit and listen to what is being narrated, a story can be constructed in the interaction between the researcher and the research participant or the participant may present a message through an artistic performance, according to Riessman (2008), who uses the terms narrative and story/account as synonyms. These may be stories told by leaders or teachers, and also by pupils in a school. Perhaps Erik and Helene experience resistance in their school, perhaps some of the teachers in a team want development while the others want stability (tension/contradiction in the factor "subject" – a primary tension, see Chapter 2). Narrative studies can be used in this situation to try to understand why these teachers resist development. Since narratives bring people's experiences to light, they may also shed light on their identities and how they perceive themselves (Creswell, 2013). Even if the research participants do not introduce themselves through a structured chronology, it could be that the researcher represents their narratives through the structure: past, present and future (Clandinin & Connelly, 2000). In narrative studies the researcher may also focus on himself/herself and write an auto-ethnography (Muncey, 2010). An auto-ethnography contains the researcher's personal history placed in a larger cultural context. This could be, for example, Erik who examines himself and how it is to function as a resource teacher in Valen school, thus in a specific school context with its culture.

According to Riessman (2008), narratives are everywhere, but not all texts or speeches are narratives. She finds that the history of a narrative started with Aristotle's analysis of Greek tragedy, and that action is imitated (mimesis). The dramatist represents events, experiences and emotions in the classic structure with a beginning, a middle section and an ending. The narrative also consists of a plot which evokes emotions and which describes something unexpected or a turning point. This means that a narrative both touches the reader and describes a development. Since narratives touch the reader, they may also have an inherent power to influence, which is also one of their purposes. The goal for narratives is that they should be strategic, functional and appropriate. Riessman gives an example: stories told about abortion, which evoke feelings of empathy across social positions and place of residence. Many forms of "texts" are now considered narratives, such as spoken, written and visual material, but which have been organised into a narrative.

5.2 *Data Collection*

Narrative research fits best when the aim is to collect detailed stories or life experiences from individuals or a small group of individuals. The researcher has to choose people with stories or experiences they want to share. The stories are called "filed texts" (Clandinin & Connelly, 2000). The researcher can write these down in a book or can record what is told. Letters sent by the participants or other public correspondence can also be used, as well as stories about the participant told by his or her family members in the data material. The data material collected in such studies is thus generally based on interview data of one kind or another. The aim of the interviews is to produce detailed narratives rather than brief answers or general statements (Riessman, 2008).

Narrative research is about creating a trusting atmosphere which invites the research participant to speak openly and in detail about events and turning points. Even if the researcher has focus on both the theory and content, he or she follows the participant's trail. The researcher must therefore relinquish control and be emotionally attentive and engaged during the interview. Having many interviews rather than just one interview will also provide the best conditions for telling stories (Riessman, 2008).

In narrative research the researcher also collects material to present the stories in their context. The contextual material the researcher collects will often deal with the participants' job and home, the culture they are part of and their historic context, both when it comes to time and location (Creswell, 2013; Riessman, 2008).

5.3 *Analysis*

According to Riessman (2008), the researcher is never neutral but always present during the entire research process in the endeavour to achieve understanding. This means that the researcher is analysing all the time, also when the transcription is being written. Some researchers think that transcribing is a technical job and let others do it. But Riessman believes that deep analyses occurs during this work, and that the researcher therefore must do the transcription him- or herself.

Riessman (2008) presents four forms of analysis: "thematic analysis", "structural analysis", "dialogic/performative analysis" and "visual analysis". In "thematic analysis" the researcher focuses on what is said or written during the data collection process. She describes this form of analysis as the most popular within narrative research and points out that this form of analysis keeps the story intact by staying focused with the participants and their narratives rather than categorising across the research participants' stories. The researcher collects data material within a theme which generates the structure of the narrative. In "the structural analysis" the researcher focuses on how the story has been told. The analysis focuses on the type of language used and the pitch and intonation of the utterances in the stories. In the third form, "the dialogic/performative analysis", the conversation is actively produced by the researcher and the research participants or actively performed by the participants through poetry or acting. In the fourth form, which is emergent, "visual analyses" are made of images, or analyses are made of words and images that are linked together.

A three-dimensional analytical approach includes analysis of the three following elements: interaction (both personal and social), continuity (past, present and future) and situation (physical locations or the research participants' places) (Clandinin & Conelly, 2000). A chronological analytical method may also be used in the analysis of narratives. The researcher then focuses on life phases (childhood, marriage, employment in working life) to develop a chronology of the person's life (Denzin, 1989).

6   Text Analysis

Qualitative text analysis is suitable when studying written documents and texts. Text analysis refers to reading and analysing printed sources and documents of various kinds, including public texts, such as national governance documents, and private texts, such as diaries, teacher biographies and blogs (Widén, 2015). Qualitative text analysis follows a long historic interpretation tradition which is called hermeneutics (Gadamer, 2012). Hermeneutics means that the researcher must attempt to understand the human perspective of people expressing themselves either verbally or in writing. The language, whether oral or written, is perceived as a text. The hermeneutic circle, or spiral, constitutes the core of a process creating understanding and meaning (Gudmundsdottir, 1997).

Widén (2015) presents three analytical dimensions for the text analysis. The first dimension refers to analysing the perceptions and purpose the originator, the writer of the text, has when writing the text. These could be texts about teachers' experiences of development activities. In the second dimension described by Widén attention is given to the form and content of the text. The focus is on the language and the text. The researcher might examine how metaphors, images and linguistic terms may have been used to describe the teachers' work. The third dimension refers to interpreting the implications of the text for settings and situations beyond the texts themselves. These may be parliamentary reports and national and local curricula which provide the framework and direction for the practice in school, or they could be textbooks.

According to Widén (2015), to answer the research questions, the researcher must obtain suitable empirical material and then categorise it. He does not specify how this categorisation should be done. Strauss and Corbin (1990) state that the constant comparative analysis method can also be used in text analysis to structure the material.

7   Conversation Analysis

Conversation analysis, often abbreviated to CA, is a detailed study of linguistic interaction (Tholander & Cekaite, 2015). CA has its origin in the understanding that language forms the world rather than that it captures what occurs in the world (Gergen, 1995; Rorty, 1989). Researchers who use this analytical method therefore first study how social actions are staged in day-to-day interaction. According to Sacks (1992), using this method, language can be analysed in detail. The intention behind this analytical method is to understand the language that arises in natural situations based on the participant perspective without the researcher having initiated the interaction, and where attention is on both what is said and how it is said. CA can be used when the empirical material consists of audio or video recordings from various conversation situations, and, according to Tholander and Cekaite (2015), it is important that the researcher transcribes the recordings him- or herself, thus listening to the recordings over and over and continuing to make new discoveries and analyses. According to Sacks (1992), transcriptions for the researcher correspond to the biologist's microscope. The main task of the researcher is to understand the utterances, not to speculate on what is going on with the participants or to assess the statements in comparison to reality or moral issues (Tholander & Cekaite, 2015).

The researcher can study turn-taking. Taking turns refers to all the procedures connected to participants speaking in turn and taking turns to speak (Sacks, Schegloff, & Jefferson, 1974). The researcher can also focus on sequential activities, that is how the conversation is structured as proximity pairs. These could for example be question – answer, greeting – greeting, proposal – rejection (Tholander & Cekaite, 2015), or they could involve interaction between teachers such as description – support. According to City, Elmore, Fiarma, and Tietel (2010), teachers usually give each other supportive statements after somebody has retold an episode from teaching in the classroom. For example, the teacher, Erik, could study how teachers talk together when giving each other feedback about stories from teaching or observed teaching. The knowledge Erik develops in such an analysis may be fed back to the teachers like a mirror reflecting how they talk. When raising awareness of the use of language though this approach, language can also be developed to "shape the world", or in this context develop the teaching in the classroom.

CHAPTER 6

Data Collection

1 Introduction

In this chapter I will present ways of collecting data. First I will describe observation as a data collection strategy, as well as various observer roles, and then I will examine how interviews can be used. I will also explain how the researcher can combine observations and interviews to find answers to research questions, and I will present a new way of using focus-group interviews where the intention is to develop the interview situation and next the setting and situation talked about. Finally, I will provide some practical advice on observations and interviews.

2 Observation as a Data Collection Strategy

Observation has been seen as the most fundamental way of collecting data (Adler & Adler, 1994). In qualitative research observation is carried out in natural situations as they play out, and the observation is therefore also called naturalistic (Angrosino & Pérez, 2000). The observation is not held in the context of a controlled experiment, and in the observation session the researcher is aware both of the human activity and the physical setting where it takes place (Angrosino & Rosenberg, 2011; Wolcott, 2008). In everyday life we are in natural settings, and we socialise with the people we observe. We are always in situations and settings which we attempt to understand and we are observing all the time. Observation is not only about seeing, but about using all our senses to perceive and understand. On a summer's day we may walk on the beach at low tide and listen to the waves rolling in. We can smell seaweed and see terns diving into the water to find food. We may pick berries from the crowberry plants hugging the weather-beaten rocks along the sea and taste them. If we are not too afraid of cold water we can take a dip in the sea and taste the salty water. In much the same way the researcher can approach school and the activity there. This is about being open to grasping what is going on, but in a research context. This is in contrast to everyday life as the researcher has a clear focus, the observations are not random: research is about focused observations (Angrosino & Pérez, 2000).

Great faith has been placed in observations. Criminal cases often hinge on witness statements to decide the verdict. Since the epistemological stance in qualitative research is that knowledge is created in the interaction between the researcher and research participants (Guba & Lincoln, 1988), observation is not an adequate way of collecting data material if used alone. When the researcher observes, his or her gaze, the etic perspective (Wolcott, 2008), is focused on the processes playing out. With his or her subjectivity and assumptions the researcher analyses and interprets what he or she grasps. Collecting empirical material where the meaning of the participants studied is not taken into consideration beyond the fact that it is the researcher who observes, analyses and interprets is insufficient in qualitative research within a constructivist paradigm. According to Angrosino and Rosenberg (2011) the goal in contemporary observation research is not to replace the classical ideal of objectivity with a total membership-driven empathy. However, they believe that the researcher's background must be considered, and that observation research is therefore more subjective than it was in the classical tradition where the objectivity principle was prevalent. Seeing oneself as a complete observer is not the way qualitative researchers want to present themselves or their research, according to Wolcott (2008).

As described above, the researcher's subjectivity and assumptions will be present in a qualitative observation, but observation and interviews will complement each other as a data collection strategy in qualitative research so that intersubjective knowledge can be constructed between the researcher and the research participants. Angrosino and Pérez (2000) state that observations may function as a context for interviews, but I, on the other hand, have experienced that interviews and observations together can mutually contribute contextual information. Observations may contribute supplementary information for the coming interviews, and the interviews for the coming observations. Observations and interviews can thus function as equal and complementary data collection strategies where both are part of the study, as in ethnographic studies and case studies.

3 Different Observer Roles

Gold (1958) has named observer roles, ranging from "complete observer" to "complete participant". Between these roles he has placed "observer-as-participant" and "participant-as-observer". In the role as "complete observer" the researcher has no connections to the situations being observed, and he or she will in no way interact with the people being observed. In the "observer-as-participant" role the researcher is mostly the observer and does not participate in the activity being observed. If researchers are observing in the classroom, however, they can respond in a friendly way to questions from pupils about who they are and what they are doing there, but not to questions about the teaching. When asked about the teaching the researcher will ask the pupils to address the teacher. The researcher is thus not part of the processes observed. In the "participant-as-observer" role the researcher assumes a clearer observer role than when he or she is a complete participant. Perhaps there are two teachers in the classroom who have agreed that one of them will assume the role of observer during part of the teaching. When the researcher is a "complete participant", he or she is part of what is being observed. Complete participants may be teachers observing their own teaching (Postholm & Jacobsen, 2011). However, it can be challenging to observe while teaching, and the teacher researcher could then possibly write down observation notes immediately after the teaching period is over, or, for example, while the pupils have been asked to write a self-evaluation in their logbooks.

In the observation context Adler and Adler (1994) have described the researcher's role in observation as a membership role. They further describe this as a "peripheral membership role" where the researcher tries to develop understanding of the research without becoming involved in the activity the core members are participating in. In an "active membership" the researcher is actively part of the observed group's important tasks. The researcher can also at times make proposals which may contribute to developing the group's actions, without tying him- or herself completely to the goals of the members. A third role described by Adler and Adler is the "complete membership role". This role comprises researchers studying processes which they already are a part of or which they join in the course of the research. This role may be compared to the role described by Gold (1958) as the "complete participant" role. This may be the role Erik assumes when, for example, he is going to study teacher collaboration in his own school.

Savin-Baden and Major (2013) use five different participant roles to describe the observer role. In the "peripheral participant role" the researcher acts as the name suggests, on the periphery of what is being observed through a webcam or two-way mirror. The researcher's goal is to remain at a distance to what is being observed, thus having the least influence possible. In the "passive participant role" the researcher is in the setting being observed. He or she is a spectator and not in interaction with the people in the setting. The researcher is a complete observer, in Gold's (1958) term. In the "balanced participant role" (Savin-Baden & Major, 2013) the researcher attempts to find a balance between the role as "outsider" and "insider", participating occasionally in the activity, more like an "observer-as-participant" (Gold, 1958); the researcher is in a "peripheral membership role" (Adler & Adler, 1994). In the "active participant role" (Savin-Baden & Major, 2013) the researcher is an active participant and has a key place or function in the setting while also observing this setting. In this role the researcher is dependent on the participants accepting that he or she takes on this role. This role is similar to the "active membership role" as described by Adler and Adler (1994). In the "complete membership role" (Savin-Baden & Major, 2013) the researcher is an active participant and also a member of the community he or she is observing. In this role the researcher has started research as an active participant in the community being studied and there is a natural reason why he or she is part of the observed setting. The researcher is a "complete participant" (Gold, 1958) or assumes a "complete membership role" (Adler & Adler, 1994), which I suggest could be Erik's role when studying teacher collaboration in his own school.

4   Interviews as a Data Collection Strategy

The word interview, from the French word "entrevue", means inter viewing, where those who participate in the interview arrive at common (inter) opinions (views). Knowledge is thus created in the interaction between researcher and research participants (Guba & Lincoln, 1988). In our everyday world we converse all the time, and we use language to communicate with each other. But the conversation is usually about cursory subjects and is rarely focused on specific areas. In the research interview, the intention is to develop knowledge connected to a specific theme, and the researcher is normally the one who leads the interview according to the research questions for the study. The research interview will therefore delve deeper into a specific theme than the spontaneous everyday conversation will. Bearing in mind that we converse all the time, we might mistakenly assume that an interview is an easy way to collect data. I have found that interviews are a challenge for the researcher, and I will examine how the researcher can develop in this situation.

Interviews normally occur face to face, but the internet has made it possible to conduct interviews even if the researcher and research participants are in different locations. Telephone, e-mail and chat software can also be used in interview situations, which means that interviews can be verbal and written based. Below I present different types of interviews, and I give examples of how these can be used when researchers would like to develop their knowledge and understanding when researching development activities while also supporting the processes in such activities.

5 Types of Interviews

Below I will first describe three interview types: the structured, the unstructured and the semi-structured interview (Fontana & Frey, 2000; Kvale & Brinkmann, 2015). Then I will present questions that can help the researcher in the interview. Even if these questions are presented before the focus-group interview (Fontana & Frey, 2000; Kamberelis & Dimitriadis, 2011), and what I call the intervening focus-group interview, this does not mean that they cannot also be used in these interviews. In the description of the interviews I will mainly focus on the semi-structured interview and the focus-group interview, as these will be most relevant for research and DWR in school.

5.1 *The Structured Interview*

In this interview the researcher asks the same questions of all the respondents and in this context the participants in the research project can be called respondents because their job is to respond to the questions. They have no influence on the interview process. The questions asked are prepared in advance with a limited set of response categories. The researcher controls the interview pace, proceeding in a standardised manner, as if the questions were the manuscript in a play. All the respondents are asked the same questions in the same order by the researcher, who also has been trained to deal with all the interview situations in the same way. The researcher must never improvise by adding response categories or changing the phrasing of the questions and must adopt a neutral role. Surveys can be defined as being this type of structured interview (Fontana & Frey, 2000).

5.2 *The Unstructured Interview*

The unstructured interview is, as the name suggests, the opposite of the structured interview. Some researchers distinguish between observation and the unstructured interview, while others believe that these forms of data collection go hand in hand (Fontana & Frey, 2000). Even though I also believe that observations and this interview type go hand in hand I still distinguish between these two data collection methods. According to Wolcott (2008), it is beneficial for the researcher to make decisions about which data collection strategies to use and how they should be used when keeping the observations and interviews separate. In the unstructured interview no questions are prepared in advance, but teachers may approach the researcher and talk about their teaching practice while the researcher is on the sidelines observing. In this talk the researcher can learn about the situation in a different way than would have been possible if he or she only observed it. The researcher can find out what the teacher was thinking about the different activities, acquire insight into why some of the pupils are working with other assignments than the others and why the pupil groups have been composed in the way they are. If there are several teachers in the classroom, they can also talk about how they distribute responsibility and how they may have planned the teaching together. For example, when Erik observes a teacher meeting in another school than his own to obtain an understanding of how these meetings are arranged, some teachers may also approach him to talk about what they think about these meetings and how they are led and prepared for. This also applies to Leona and Leander when they carry out research on teaching progress and teacher teams.

5.3   *The Semi-Structured Interview*

The aim of the semi-structured interview is to understand the participants' perspective (Kvale & Brinkmann, 2015). Knowledge is created in the interaction between the researcher and the points of view of the interviewees. The researcher has prepared themes and proposed questions in advance but is not obligated to ask these questions or introduce the themes in a particular order. The questions are asked where it is natural to insert them into the interview. The researcher is also open to the research participants introducing themes that have not been anticipated. The construction of knowledge that occurs in the course of the interview can also lead the researcher to ask unprepared questions. Thus there is an on-going exchange between deduction and induction as described in Chapter 3, which is called abduction (Alvesson & Sköldberg, 2009). Both parties in the interview attempt to understand and perceive meaning in what is said. In this type of interview the analysis is continuous, which is why the researcher wants to ask different questions based on what is said so he or she can really grasp and understand actions and thoughts raised in the interview. This type of interview is often preferred in case studies, ethnographic studies, phenomenological studies and narrative studies.

6   Questions That Help the Researcher Achieve Understanding

Questions that help the researcher achieve understanding during the interview are: "the questions in the interview guide", "follow-up questions" and "probing questions" (Rubin & Rubin, 2005). The questions in the interview guide are prepared before the interview to cover the areas which the main research question and the sub-questions frame. Follow-up questions are used to obtain explanations connected to the theme, concepts or events the research participant introduces in the course of the interview. Probes or probing questions help the researcher to keep the research focused on the theme being studied. They indicate the desired depth in the interview, and they are asked to obtain explanations. The interview guide questions help the researcher to answer the research questions, while the follow-up questions and the probing questions add depth, details and nuances in the interview.

6.1   *Follow-up Questions*

Follow-up questions are asked about the research participant's response in the interview. The researcher listens carefully to what the informant says and follows this by asking questions to achieve depth, rich detail and more nuanced responses. Follow-up questions are asked during the interview as it is taking place but could also be asked in a subsequent interview after the researcher has transcribed the original interview, carried out the initial analyses and then realises that some statements should have been followed up. The researcher will often follow up something that appears to be new and unexpected or interesting for the research questions. Statements that are felt to be inconsistent can also be addressed more (Rubin & Rubin, 2005). When the researcher asks follow-up questions, they will address directly what has been stated in the interview. If the researcher carries out a follow-up interview to obtain answers to the questions asked, reference will normally be made to the previous interview with a summary of what was said then before asking the follow-up question.

It may be easier to follow up what has been said than to ask follow-up questions that relate to emotions. If the research participants have mentioned activities that can be compared, for example lesson study and action learning as methods for the teacher's learning, the researcher may ask the informant to compare these methods. Questions can be asked when the original statements are found to be inconsistent. If the research participants offer a conclusion, it may be useful to ask whether this generalisation is applicable under all circumstances to dig in depth into what has been said: "Does it always happen this way?" If the researcher feels that the participant is hinting at something, this is virtually an invitation to follow up what has been said, for example with a statement like: "I'm not sure if the mathematics teachers should cooperate with the arts and crafts teacher". The researcher may also play the devil's advocate and ask challenging questions. Such questions may coax the participant into offering more arguments than what was found in the original statement (inspired by Rubin & Rubin, 2005, with my own examples).

6.2   *Probing Questions*

Probing questions help the researcher to keep the conversation going while also digging in-depth into what was said. While follow-up questions can be asked in a later interview, probing questions must be asked during the interview as they encourage the informant to elaborate on what was just said or to give additional explanations. Probing questions keep the research participant talking about the theme of the interview, elaborating on an idea and filling in pieces that are missing so that the statements can be understood, or they can aim to encourage the informant to clarify what was just said. The researcher should ask a limited number of probing questions in the interview and must also be cautious when asking them so that the situation does not appear to be confrontational. One way of doing this could be to remain silent for some seconds so that the research participant feels that he or she is expected to continue speaking, or the researcher could nod or make a gesture signalling that the participant should continue (Rubin & Rubin, 2005).

Probing questions signal to the research participant that he or she should continue speaking and give more detailed answers. The researcher may say "Mmm, hmm", "and then", or simply use a short pause, leaving the silence to be filled by the participant. Probing questions could be, for example:
– Can you give me an example of this?
– Do you have more examples of this?
– Can you tell me more about this?
– Can you give me a more detailed description of what happened?
– What do you mean by that?
– This was interesting, please tell me more?
– Can you tell me step by step what happened?
– How did you reach this conclusion?

Questions for eliciting emotions could be:
– How did you react when …?
– Which reactions did you have when …?
– What did you feel when …?
– What did you experience …?

The researcher may also ask a probing question to check whether he or she has understood what has been said: "Could you please say that again, I couldn't quite follow you", or the researcher can repeat what the participant said in his or her own words and ask whether it has been understood correctly. As mentioned above one of the intentions of probing questions is also to keep the interview focused on the theme of the conversation. If the research participant strays outside this area in the interview, the researcher can say: "This was interesting, but should we move back to the theme of the interview?" The researcher should not ask leading questions which would give the researcher the answers he or she wants, but in this case the point is to lead the research participant back on the track of the theme of the interview.

6.3   Model Questions

Rubin and Rubin (2005, pp. 142–145) present three models which each depict possible interview procedures: "opening the locks", "tree and branch", and "river and channel". The aim of the opening-the-locks interview is to get the research participant to talk for a long period so the researcher can gain an overview of what is going on to determine what should be examined in depth at a later stage. In the tree-and-branch interview the researcher divides the research questions into equal parts or themes, and each of these is covered with questions in the interview guide. The trunk of the tree is the main research question and the branches represent the questions in the interview guide. The researcher then attempts to ask all the questions and pursue them further by asking follow-up and probing questions. In the river-and-channel interview the researcher chooses to explore an idea, a concept or a case and pursue this focus wherever it leads. This may mean that the researcher pursues one follow-up question so that not all the questions in the interview guide are answered. The researcher chooses a channel to the river and follows it to explore issues which the channel symbolises in detail and depth. If the researcher wants answers to the main research question, the tree-and-branch model is the best to follow. An example of an interview guide focusing on the main research question is presented in Appendix 2.

6.4   Questions in Concrete Research

When Helene and Erik are to understand the current situation (see Figure 2.4, chapter 2: the expansive learning cycle) in the school before they develop goals and the direction of the planned development project together with all the teachers (new model, stage 3 in the same figure), they can both observe and interview teachers and leaders. If the development question is "How can the communication in the interaction between teachers and between teachers and pupils be developed so that the pupils have better learning outcome and the relationships between all the parties are improved?", then Helene and Erik can carry out a micro-ethnographic study to understand the communication between the teachers. This could also be the focus for Erik's study of teacher teams. If the teachers state that they would like to cooperate better, follow-up questions can be asked for an in-depth examination of this point to acquire more detailed descriptions of how this cooperation has been over time. Probing questions could then be asked according to these descriptions to find out how this cooperation is currently functioning. The probing questions could be:

"Can you give a specific description of how you cooperate in the team when you are planning teaching?", "That was interesting. Can you elaborate on this point?", or "What do you mean by that?" Such questions can encourage the research participants to elaborate on what has already been said so that the researcher can obtain a comprehensive description of the cooperation situation. The researcher could also ask the teachers to outline a cooperation situation to find out more about relevant actions and emotions. To obtain rich data material, the researcher can also ask the research participants to describe additional examples of cooperation.

6.5 Clarification Questions

If the teacher who is being interviewed is somewhat ambiguous in his or her answers so that Helene and Erik do not know whether the teacher wants to cooperate and improve communications or would like to work more individually, they can ask a "clarification question". A direct or concrete question can be asked of the teachers in a team as to how they experience the cooperation in their team. Perhaps the teachers have observed their teaching mutually and given each other feedback afterwards. Probing questions for the teacher could then be: "How did you react when you received feedback?", "What was the reaction to the feedback?", "What did you feel when you received the feedback?" or "How did you experience the feedback?" Clarification questions are the fourth way of asking questions, and as the name suggests, they may help the researcher to clarify what has been said. Such clarification questions may be: "Do I understand you correctly when you say that cooperation contributes to your own learning?" or "Does this mean that you believe that the communication with your fellow teachers does help you to learn more?"

6.6 Different Methodological Approaches and Questions

As mentioned above, the researcher can ask different types of questions during an interview. But this means that the researcher must be present and alert so that he or she can ask questions that will provide in-depth information (Postholm, 2013). A researcher in a micro-ethnographic study, a case study or a narrative study can also ask such questions in subsequent interviews, as these studies continue over a period of time. The researcher can then listen to and preferably transcribe the interview to be well prepared for the next round with follow-up questions in hand.

When it comes to interviews in a phenomenological study, the researcher often conducts only one interview with each research participant. In Chapter 5 I recommended that if there are three participants in a phenomenological study they should be selected according to the same criteria and same context.

In this way their essence could be described and recognised in similar settings with similar people. When an essence is to be crystallised based on three interviews, the participants will also have to make statements about the same issue so that its essence can be described across the three interviews. This means that the participants should be asked to make statements about the same things. The researcher prepares a semi-structured interview with topics and perhaps some questions, but during the second interview the second interviewee might touch on matters that have not be dealt with by the first interviewee. If the point is to have statements about the same thing, the researcher will need to conduct a follow-up interview with the first participant to touch on the same matter. This also means that the researcher must be clear right from the start as to whether it will be possible to conduct a follow-up interview, which could for example be carried out as a telephone interview.

6.7 The Focus-Group Interview

Normally six to ten people will participate in a focus-group interview which is led by the researcher, or moderator, as she or he may also be called (Chrzanowska, 2002). The researcher presents the topic to be discussed and leads the discussion. The interview guide for such an interview is usually similar to the one a researcher would formulate for a semi-structured interview. The questions presented above can also be used in the focus-group interview, but the researcher is not as active here in asking questions as when facing one person in an interview situation. The intention is that the interview participants should do as much of the talking as possible, and the researcher's task is to nudge the dialogue onto topics he or she wants the group members to talk about. The researcher must also create a good and open atmosphere in the interview situation so that all the participants are willing to make statements, thus opening for many points of view on the subject in focus (Chrzanowska, 2002). The goal is not that the focus-group interview participants should reach consensus or find solutions to the questions discussed, but the researcher may also find that the participants have a common or collective idea about the topic in question (Kamberelis & Dimitriadis, 2011). The researcher may then use "the teachers", "the leaders" or "the pupils" as common designations when presenting the utterances and opinions of the participants in the research report. In the interview, counter arguments may be given for statements the researcher initially understands as agreement. Thus the focus-group interview allows the participants to make statements collectively or in their individual voices (Kamberelis & Dimitriadis, 2011). Kamberelis and Dimitriadis (2011) have described the function of the focus-group interview in connection with the participants focusing on specific cases and issues, constructing knowledge and strategies together to improve their situations and circumstances. However, in the traditional focus-group interview the intention has been to gather information without necessarily having the aim of improving the conditions or situations in the study (Fontana & Frey, 2000). In my view, focus-group interviews may also be used in school to contribute to changing practice both in and out of the classroom. I call this type of interview the intervening focus-group interview.

6.8 Intervening Focus-Group Interviews

In an individual interview the participant is separated from his or her social context. On the other hand, the researcher can invite people who work together on a day-to-day basis to take part in an "intervening focus-group interview" so they are in the same social context. The invited participants could be teacher teams and leader teams in school. In a traditional focus-group interview Helene could interview a leader team in another school to acquire an understanding of how they lead development activities, and then bring the insight from this interview back to her own school. Erik could also interview a teacher team in another school to learn more about the cooperation processes in this team. Helene and Erik could also use an intervening focus-group interview to create a dialogue that contributes to development in their own school. A DWR group consisting of teacher educators and student teachers in interaction with teachers and leaders may also use this form of interview in DWR. An intervening focus-group interview will then function as a "development interview". Often, when teachers are to give responses to each other, after observing each other's teaching, for example, they may be kind in their feedback and give each other positive feedback (City et al., 2010; Junge, 2012). In intervening focus-group interviews questions like the ones presented in the preceding section may be used. As I see it, it is also possible to be in an amicable dialogue while also challenging and giving advice about what has been said. According to Bjørndal (2011) people who have established a trusting relationship and good relations to those receiving advice are in a position to be able to give advice. If there is a trusting relationship between the parties it is also easier to reject advice if its usefulness in the situation is doubted. Having a trusting relationship and good relations will make it possible to accept this. This means that researchers coming from outside the environment must understand the importance of developing good relations to teachers and leaders in school. In her capacity as the principal in a development project Helene could perhaps choose to be more present into the classrooms and observe before speaking with the teachers afterward, but she may find that it will take time before the teachers feel confident enough to have her in their classroom. In his capacity as a teacher, Eric may be in a better position to observe classrooms with subsequent reflections in an intervening focus-group interview, as he is working closer to the teachers, and also teaches, thus experiencing challenges and envisioning opportunities the other teachers might also be familiar with.

7 Connection between Interview and Observation

In the introduction to the chapter I stated that observations and interviews may function as equal and complementary data-collection strategies. This applies in particular to studies stretching over time, such as case studies and micro-ethnographic studies. The researcher often starts the research process with an introductory interview with, for example, the principal in a leader team, the main informant of a teacher team or the teacher who is to teach in a classroom. In this interview the researcher asks questions that contribute background information, which may be about the school, participation in programmes and the interviewee's personal work situation and experience. In an initial interview, the researcher can also ask the research participant to state more about the planning and thinking behind the meeting or teaching session about to be observed. This may help the researcher to prepare for the observation. During the observation itself the researcher may write down notes, preferably in a logbook. An example of an observation note is shown in Figure 6.1.

The pages in the observation book can be divided into two columns where the left column is for descriptions of what has been observed. The main research thesis and the research questions frame the observation, but in individual observations the researcher may decide to have a narrow focus in the observation within the overarching frame. Even if the researcher has a clear focus for his or her observations, the subjectivity of the researcher will influence what is selected and noted. When observing the processes, the researcher will have his or her experiences and theories that will form the assumptions that will be taken into the research field. The researcher's subjectivity will thus have impact on what is observed and what is found to be important. This means that the description in the left column will never be objective or value neutral.

In the right-hand column the researcher can enter preliminary analyses and interpretations, as well as questions that may surface during the observation. The researcher will also have formulated some questions in the observation session that are intended for the next interview. In the course of the interview the researcher may learn more about the opinions of the participants in relation to what has been observed. What emerges in the interviews may help the researcher to develop his or her understanding of the topic of the research.

DATA COLLECTION 81

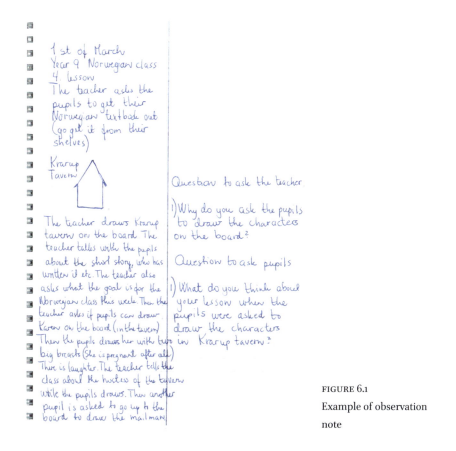

FIGURE 6.1
Example of observation note

In this process the researcher will alternate between his or her assumptions and the data material. The understanding developed according to the individual parts (observation and interview) may help the researcher to develop a holistic understanding of the area under study. The researcher is here in the hermeneutic spiral, a process which helps create understanding and meaning (Gudmundsdottir, 1997).

8   Practical Advice

8.1   *In Connection with Observation*

Before the research and the observation session start it is very important for the researcher to read theory relating to the topic being studied. The theory helps the researcher to focus in the observation session and thus to pick up and zoom in on pieces of a holistic reality that are written down on an ongoing basis. However, the theory may also blind the researcher in his or her observation. An observation carried out by a researcher with another set of theory glasses, but with the same focus in the same setting and situation, may pick up on and thus emphasise completely different conditions. The following quotation captures this well: "A way of seeing is, indeed, also a way of not seeing" (Burke, 1935, p. 70).

Before the observation starts, the researcher should decide which observer role to assume, and keep to that role. Then everyone who participates in the activity knows what the observer's role is and can act accordingly. If Erik wants to observe in the classroom and states that he will act the role of "observer-as-participant", and informing his participants what that implies, the teacher in the classroom will then know that he is not an extra teacher in the classroom. The observer role assumed by Erik should also be something the pupils are aware of so that they also know that they should act in relation to Erik as the researcher and not as Erik the teacher. When Leona is to observe a teaching programme, it is also important that she clarifies her role to all those concerned.

Audio and video recordings may be useful in classroom observations and in observations of meetings. While the researcher might be able to make some notes during the observation, it will be difficult to catch everything. The equipment the researcher uses will also depend on what the observation is focusing on. Before the observation the researcher should familiarise him- or herself with the recording equipment so that attention is on the activity and not on the equipment. If the researcher is interested in what is said, i.e. verbal response, an audio recorder can be used. This could, for example, be used when teachers and pupils are talking, when pupils are talking in a group or when teachers or leaders are talking together in a team. If the researcher is interested in capturing both verbal and non-verbal expressions, a video camera can be used. A video recording also makes it possible for the researcher to experience the situation again and again, thus continuing the observation and analysis. In would appear that in the research situation video recording can be experienced as more disturbing and challenging for the research participants than audio recording. The researcher should therefore consider which aids are useful and necessary for getting answers to his or her questions. A video recording could, however, be a good starting point and the focus point for an interview with the research participants who have been recorded.

8.2   *In the Context of Interviews*

As I wrote in the introduction, it can be challenging to conduct interviews. How the interview itself develops and which information the researcher is left with after the interview depend on the preparations. It is essential that the researcher studies the topic well before the interview. Reading theory about the area in focus for the interview will help the researcher to prepare topics and questions for the interview guide. However, the researcher's theories and subjectivity will colour the content of the conversation in much the same way as with the data material from the observation that is created in the interaction between the researcher and the activity that has been observed. The researcher will benefit from carrying out a test interview to determine how the questions and answers open for dialogue, preferably as a role play. It can also be a good learning experience to transcribe this interview to hear how you as the researcher ask questions and follow up the answers.

Audio and video recordings may be used in the interview context. Before the interview, the researcher should, as when having an observation session, consider which type of equipment is necessary and become familiar with the equipment before it is to be used so attention is on what is said in the interview. Conducting an interview demands full concentration from the researcher to be able to ask follow-up questions, probing questions and clarifying questions during the conversation. If the participants are to experience the interview as a non-frightening situation, they should be allowed to choose the location for the interview. It may also be a good idea to start with a warm-up conversation, with coffee and pastry perhaps. The length of the interview should also be determined in advance, and the researcher should stay within the allotted time. An individual interview normally does not take more than an hour, and a focus-group interview 90 minutes. If some questions remain, the researcher should rather agree on a follow-up interview when time is up, or even preferably agree in advance on whether a follow-up interview is possible if the allotted time turns out to be inadequate.

At the start of the interview the researcher may ask the participants about education and work experience and other contextual information for the content of the interview. For the conversation to flow as smoothly as possible, it is not a given that the questions or topics listed in the interview guide should be asked in order. This also means that the researcher must be well versed in the interview guide so that he or she knows if a question further down the list in the interview guide has already been addressed, or that a question or topic planned for the end of the interview should be introduced earlier in the conversation than planned. To make sure that the interviewee does not feel that the interview is a technical listing of questions and topics, the researcher should plan good segues between topics and questions. As I wrote in the introduction, all the participants in an interview try to create meaning from what is said. If the researcher suddenly starts writing, the participant(s) may feel that what has just been said is particularly important, whilst the other statements were not interesting enough to be noted down. My advice is that the researcher should trust the recorder to capture what is said, and rather stay in the conversation without writing. Perhaps the researcher would like to note down a question that surfaces in the course of the interview before it is forgotten, but if so, the participants should be informed about this possibility. Then they will not start wondering what the researcher is writing and why.

CHAPTER 7

Analysing the Data Material Using the Constant Comparative Analysis Method and D-Analysis

1   Introduction

In our day-to-day lives we are continuously trying to understand what is going on around us. When we relax on a park bench we can hear the birds singing, we can smell summer beginning to blossom and we notice and perhaps try to understand small parts of the lives of the people who either pass by quickly or saunter past the bench we are sitting on. Why do some people seem to dress more for a cold spring day when the warming sun is in fact shining from clear blue skies? Have they had a busy morning? Why are some people rushing? Are they late for an appointment? These types of more or less random questions may come to mind when we think about our impressions of the people we watch as they pass by. Unlike us, who are sitting on the park bench, the researcher has a specific focus for his or her data collection and collects and analyses data systematically.

The intention of qualitative analytical methods is first to sort data material collected in a study to make the material comprehensible (Merrian, 2009). I call this type of analysis where material is structured and made report-friendly "descriptive analysis" (Postholm, 2010). Charmaz (2014) claims that this phase in the analysis is the skeleton for the further analysis in the research. In many cases this is about looking for patterns so that the material can be sorted into categories or under different themes. The data material in qualitative studies is often comprehensive, where the analytical process is often about gaining a workable overview of this material so that it can be presented to others in a written text.

While some may think this means that the analysis commences when all the collected material has been transcribed and exists in written form, they would be wrong. The analysis begins immediately when the researcher is in the field, in a dialogue aiming for development of the practice field or in an interview where the material is being collected. In an observation situation, the researcher attempts to understand what is going on, noting both what occurs and how this is immediately understood. In a dialogue aiming for development, the researcher also continuously analyses to ask constructive questions and give suitable feedback and comments to support and challenge practitioners. The analysis begins immediately when the researcher is in the field or in the interview situation where the material is being collected. In an observation situation the researcher attempts to understand what is going on, noting down both what occurs and how this is immediately understood. An essential part of the interview situation is that the researcher is present in it, so that immediate analyses or interpretations can be made in the interview, which then constitute the basis for asking follow-up questions. A qualitative researcher should therefore always have a notebook or logbook close at hand, both during the data collection period and when analysing the transcribed material so that initial thoughts and preliminary analyses and interpretations can be written down. Another way to do this is to use a voice recorder to record thoughts, analyses and interpretations.

In Chapter 5 I have presented different approaches in qualitative methods and the analytical methods relating to these. These were analytical methods in case studies, ethnography, phenomenology, narrative studies, text analysis and conversation analysis. Strauss and Corbin (1990, 1998) and Corbin and Strauss (2008) have developed the constant comparative analysis method, where they claim that this way of analysing data material can be used in all studies, including case studies, micro-ethnographic studies, phenomenological studies and narrative studies. According to the authors, this analytical approach can also be applied when analysing a text, such as curricula, white papers or research articles. This analytical method can also be used when carrying out research and collecting data material in DWR. The constant comparative method helps the researcher to structure the data into categories. Within each category, the researcher can also study discourse or communication using discourse analyses (D-analysis) (Middleton, 2010) to understand how development unfolds. Since the constant comparative analysis method is useful in several approaches, I will present a thorough description of it here before I present an example using D-analysis (Middleton, 2010).

2   The Point of Departure and Purpose of the Constant Comparative Analysis Method

Grounded theory as a methodology was originally developed by two sociologists, Barney Glaser and Anselm Strauss. Strauss came from the University of Chicago, which had a long history of qualitative research. Strauss was influenced by Interactionists and Pragmatists, such as Georg Herbert Mead, John Dewey and Herbert Blumer. This background contributed to the method they developed, which emphasises that researchers should go into the field to understand what is going on, the importance of theory grounded in reality, the active role of persons shaping the world they live in and the focus on change and processes. Glaser came from another tradition at Columbia University, influenced by Paul Lazarsfeld and quantitative methods. When Glaser later conducted qualitative analyses, he saw the need for systematic sets of procedures. The Columbia tradition also emphasised empirical research in conjunction with development theory, and both research traditions were directed at producing research that would be of use to professional or lay audiences (Strauss & Corbin, 1990). Grounded theory (GT), which is often referred to as the constant comparative analysis method (Glaser & Strauss, 1967, pp. 101–116) – the term I will use – is therefore appropriate to use when analysing data material in DWR and in combination with D-analysis.

Even though the constant comparative analysis method has been developed within grounded theory, it can, as mentioned above, be used in different approaches (Strauss & Corbin, 1990, 1998; Creswell, 2013). Basically the aim of the analytical method is to develop a theory grounded on the collected material. This is no longer so clear-cut in the method books, a point I will return to later. A well-constructed theory must satisfy the following criteria: fit, understanding, generality and control. If the theory is faithful in presenting the realities in the field or the phenomenon being studied and is deduced from the collected material, then it fits. Because it represents reality, it may also be understandable for the people who have been studied and others in the same setting. If the data and the interpretations are sufficiently abstract, the theory should also be applicable in other similar contexts than the one studied. The constructed theory should also give direction with respect to how to act in situations and settings like the one being studied (Glaser & Strauss, 1967, pp. 237–259).

The constant comparative analysis method has systematic procedures for how the analytical process should be carried out, but this process is not a mechanical or automated process. The researcher must be present with his or her creativity in the analytical process. The researcher's creativity is found in the naming of categories and all the questions asked in the analytical process. The researcher's creativity is also challenged when he or she continuously compares data to make discoveries.

3   The Importance of Theory When Using the Constant Comparative Analysis Method

In the constant comparative analysis method theoretical sensitivity is a key concept referring to the researcher's personal qualities and how he or she manages to analyse, understand and give meaning to the collected data material. This is done by using concepts rather than concrete terms or themes. The researcher's theoretical sensitivity depends on his or her previous experiences and reading of theory. Theory helps to sensitise the researcher to the meaning of what is studied. If the researcher has experience from the field studied, he or she will manage to gain insights into what is being studied more quickly than a person without such experience. For example, a teacher working as a researcher will probably understand what occurs in the classroom more quickly than a car mechanic. Personal experience may be helpful in research in the same way that professional experience is. If a researcher who has children is doing research in the classroom, it will probably be easier to understand how children perceive the activity in this classroom. In research, as elsewhere, the saying "practice makes perfect" holds true. The more a researcher collects and analyses data material, the better he or she will also understand the setting, situation or phenomenon studied, and the insights into how analytical processes unfold will also increase in accordance with the experience gained.

The sensitivity developed in the research does not only helps the researcher to use professional and personal experiences in a prescient manner, but also benefits the theory. It helps the researcher to see the research situation and the data material in new ways, and to explore the possibilities the material provides for developing a theory. However, while the researcher uses his or her sensitivity to see opportunities, it is also important that he or she deal with the actual conditions. To be able to do so, Strauss and Corbin (1990, 1998) propose that researchers should ask themselves the following questions: What is going on here? Does what I appear to see fit with the reality of the data? During the research process, the researcher should treat his or her personal analyses with scepticism and consider them as a preliminary part of an on-going process.

Within the framework of the research question the researcher will consider the data material according to assumptions developed from professional and personal experiences as well as from reading theory. Some of these can be discarded, while others will be confirmed when working with the data material. This material may also reveal unexpected conditions, meaning that the researcher will have to read new theory or dig deeper into already absorbed theory to analyse and understand the data material. This has been shown in Figure 3.3 in Chapter 3. In this way, the research process will continue to go back and forth between data collection, data analysis and theory, which is read and applied in the analyses (Postholm, 2010).

As described above, theory can stimulate the researcher's sensitivity to the data material and how this can form new theory. Theory can also describe situations and present concepts the researcher may find useful in his or her study. The next step will then be to determine whether the concepts and the relations between them are also relevant for the study being conducted. If so, the researcher will search for instances in his or her own data where these concepts will be relevant. Perhaps Dewey's concept of experience and Vygotsky's zone of proximal development theory will be important concepts for researchers when trying to understand how they can facilitate for teachers' learning and development, or for understanding practices in school. Theory may also help the researcher generate questions to ask the research participants. The researcher's theoretical stance will thus influence how the data material is collected and understood. A researcher grounded in socio-cultural theory will focus on mediated actions in the analysis (Wertsch, 1998), while a researcher grounded in CHAT will use the activity system as the unit of analysis (Engeström, 1999). When the analysis has been completed and it is time is to present the findings in written form, the researcher may choose to refer to existing theory and research to support his or her own findings (Strauss & Corbin, 1990).

The researcher's intention may also be to develop existing theory. This means studying how this theory can be applied in new and similar situations in relation to the context the theory was developed in. The existing theory will contribute sensitising concepts (Strauss & Corbin, 1990, p. 51) to the researcher regarding the new data material collected. Based on the findings from this study the original theory may be corrected, refined or modified to fit the specific situations studied (Strauss & Corbin, 1990, 1998). According to Strauss and Corbin (1990, 1998), a distinction must be made between theme and concept. Theme describes actions or interactions, while concepts are more abstract and involve an interpretation. The label "reading documents" is descriptive, while "collecting information" is a more abstract concept. Theories are developed in the analytical process that is based on the data material.

The constant comparative analysis method does not normally start with categories that have already been developed, in other words taken from already existing theory. This could undermine the development of new theoretical formulations. If the researcher decides to step into his or her research with categories developed beforehand, this may be done to give them new meaning or new content (Strauss & Corbin, 1990, p. 50). The constant comparative analysis method can also be used to analyse theories or documents (Strauss & Corbin, 1990; Corbin & Strauss, 2008). I used this method when writing a review of teachers' professional development (Postholm, 2012, 2018a).

The third edition of Strauss and Corbin's book was published in 2008, this time with Corbin as the first author. Strauss had passed away when this edition appeared, but Corbin has included him as the second author since many of their shared understandings were included in the third edition and she states that the book is a modernisation of the two previous editions. She believes that theory construction is no longer the only way to develop new knowledge Instead, rich and thick descriptions and the intention of promoting change can be goals for research, similar to theory construction. She describes research as a good way of mixing art with science and interpretation in a complex adventure story. Many understandings can be constructed from the same data material, and she points out the importance of the development of concepts. Her rationale for this is that concepts help people to understand their life situation better, and concepts generate a language that can be used as the point of departure for discussion, and hence for the development of a shared understanding. Corbin also maintains that it is up to the researcher to decide which research to conduct, that is, whether it should end in a description or as a theory. However, according to Corbin, the researcher must clarify the aim of the research, pointing out that if the researcher is to develop a theory, he or she must refer to explanations that are more than descriptions structured into different themes.

4   Analytical Procedures in the Constant Comparative Analysis Method

The analysis starts immediately when the researcher begins to read documents, is in the research field or conducts an interview. How the first material that has been collected is understood is also important for how the data collection continues. This initial understanding affects how new documents are read and as well as the focus in the subsequent observations, interviews, and dialogues focusing on development. The researcher does not begin this process directly on the transcriptions before all the material has been collected; rather, the analysis is on-going. In the data collection phase, the researcher makes notes in the logbook to remember the preliminary analyses. In this phase questions are already being asked about the collected material, and comparisons are being made. What do the observations reveal? How should what is said in the interviews be understood? How can the planning documents in the school be understood? What do the data sources tell me? Do they say the same things? Are there similarities or dissimilarities in what they say? In this phase the researcher analyses the whole interview, dialogues, observation or document that has been read before continuing with data collection.

In the editions from 1990 and 1998 Strauss and Corbin describe the analytical process in three stages: "open coding", "axial coding" and "selective coding".

According to the authors, coding refers to the analysis of data, where the data material is structured and labelled by using concepts. In the open coding phase, the main categories are developed, in the axial coding phase, the sub-categories are developed and in the selective coding phase, the core category is developed. In the selective coding phase, all the categories are related to each other, so the bits can be assembled into a whole and the researcher can answer the main thesis of the research. What is the core of the study? What is it about?

Throughout the entire analytical process the researcher remains open to what the data material means. Strauss and Corbin (1990, 1998) point out that there is no sharp dividing line between these three coding processes, and the researcher keeps alternating between these three stages throughout the entire analysis. Even if the analysis has been ongoing since the first moment of data collection, the researcher does not start to analyse the transcriptions until all the material has been transcribed. When it comes to transcription, Strauss and Corbin (1990, 1998) recommend that this is done with the collected material before new data is collected. The analyses of the first interviews and the first field notes will help in the next interviews and analyses. I also recommend that the researchers do the transcriptions because they will also analyse the material while transcribing. The researcher should therefore maintain a separate log, or another file on the computer, to write down these immediate analyses and interpretations. From experience I know that these glimpses of understanding may vanish as quickly as they come.

In the "open coding phase" the data material is studied, compared, given terms and categorised. When the collected material is transcribed from speech to text, the researcher can prepare broad left and right margins to allow ample space for writing comments. This applies to the interviews, but the researcher can also code and categorise observations written in a book or observation protocol. The researcher copies the pages in this book, coding and categorising directly in the copied field notes. This means that the researcher will always have an original that can be copied again if the analysis has to be done over again. This may be necessary if the researcher sees that much of the material cannot be sorted into a category. The researcher can note the codes or labels on the right side in the transcriptions and put the categories on the left side. This is shown in Table 7.1.

There are three ways of carrying out open coding. For example, the researcher can analyse the transcribed interview line by line. This way of proceeding may be compared to analysing a poem line by line through each stanza. Such analysis is obviously quite laborious if there is a large and comprehensive amount of data material. Another way is to analyse is to code each

TABLE 7.1 Visualisation of a coding and categorisation process

Type of leadership	Leader 3: This gives us the chance to continue building. We don't need to finish this when the project is done. We can simply continue. If we have focus on it, but then we need to keep it on the front burner and keep putting in on the agenda, so we don't forget about it when the project is over. I think it'll be quite easy to continue it.	The leader does not have the key Keep the work on the front burner But the leader takes initiatives
Type and scope	Leader 1: So this was probably a good point in time for us. As I say, when we summed up the year down there, it was that these long days were a little too left to chance, it was like, oh sure, that's what we're doing today, we had no plans for it, there was a wish, you know, to have something more connected. It was, seeing it like that, a good point in time. It was not good last year, and the year before, not good enough, it wasn't.	Good time for start-up
Scope of leadership	Researcher: Why is it important that all the leaders and all the teachers have participated in the project? Leader 3: I think this has been crucial, because I don't see that just anybody could do this with the school. For me it would have been meaningless, really. Perhaps mostly based on what I have read about doing development projects. Because I don't have that much experience	All the leaders and teachers take part
Leaders and teachers learn together	Leader 2: A common platform, where we read the same, prepare the same, that's something that includes everyone. Leader 3: Yes, as long as the whole staff is in it, the whole leadership team has to be included because we each have our Year group we are responsible for. Leader 1: Yes, if they don't see us as one entity here it would have gone badly, there's no doubt about that.	

sentence or paragraph. In this way the codes cover larger units and the data material will therefore be easier to work with. A third way to carry out open coding is to analyse a document in its entirety, an observation or an interview, where the researcher asks what appears to be happening here: "What is this a case of?"

Already during the data collection process the researcher can name categories which are found to be important according to the material, but while also being aware that these are preliminary categories and names. However, it is still important to name the preliminary categories so that the researcher can start analysing them. In the open coding phase during which the transcriptions are worked on, the categories are also considered to be preliminary and can eventually be given a more appropriate name. This is all about structuring the data material to facilitate a more manageable overview. The fruit department in a grocery store is a good metaphor for this analytical process. The individual types of fruit are given their name or label, but all can be placed in the category fruit. Fruit is a more abstract concept than the different types of fruit with their individual names. All the categories should be given a more abstract term than the codes or labels applied.

"Axial coding" is about making connections between a category and its sub-categories (Strauss & Corbin, 1990, 1998). This means that the researcher structures the collected data material into a category by asking when, why and under what circumstances did this category materialise, how and what does it lead to? Strauss and Corbin (1990, 1998) describe a paradigm model as the point of departure for axial coding. The following factors are part of it: (a) causal circumstances, (b) the phenomenon, (c) context, (d) intervening circumstances, (e) action/interaction strategies and (f) consequences. If, for example, the "phenomenon" is school-based competence development, the "causal circumstance" is that the national authorities in Norway implemented a national programme in 2013 in which all lower secondary school and schools with a lower secondary level had the opportunity to participate. The intention was to allow the pupils were to experience mastery, to be more motivated and to have better learning outcome (Norwegian Directorate for Education and Training, 2012). The context represents a specific set of characteristics relating to the phenomenon, in this case school-based competence development. In this connection the "context" was that the work should be led by the school leader in each school, that each school would receive support from teacher educators from the university and college sector and that the main focus was to be on classroom management, reading, writing and numeracy. Other prominent topics in the programme were assessment for learning and organisational development. "Intervening circumstances" in this work could be the school leader's ability to lead collective development processes in the school, the school owner's (local or county authorities) support in the development processes, the quality of the collaboration between the university and college sector and the school or the ability of the teachers to cooperate. They could also be the cultures and structures in the school while the project was running. These intervening circumstances could in turn affect the "actions" and "interactions" that were introduced to attain the stipulated goals. These actions and interactions then had impact on the outcome for leaders and teachers, which in turn could influence the pupils' learning as facilitated for in the school-based competence development ("consequences").

The main thesis for the pilot project (2012/2013) was the following: "How can school-based competence development contribute to learning in school and in teacher education?" The data material was collected in interviews of teacher educators in three university and college institutions, in leader and teacher groups in three schools in different municipalities connected to these three university and college institutions, and from the school owners in each of the three municipalities (Postholm et al., 2013). The analysis of the material resulted in the development of the categories shown in Figure 7.1.

The main categories developed were "Leadership at the school level", "Use of tools and artefacts", "Cooperation between teacher educators, school owners and school leaders" and "Cooperation between teacher educators and other teacher educators, and between teacher educators and national centres". As can be seen in the figure, "Experience sharing" was highlighted in a separate box, as it became a very important tool in the process. The sub-categories were developed by asking when, why and under what circumstances this category surfaced as well as how and what it leads to. For each category, the sub-categories have been given the designations "Type", "Scope", "Arena" and "Experiences". All these designations describe properties of the categories that may then be dimensioned on a scale. I will use the main category "Use of tools and artefacts" to exemplify this. "Type" refers to the tools and artefacts that are used to carry out goal-directed actions in the cooperation process. "Scope" refers to the use of tools and artefacts, which can be distributed on a continuum from used much to used little. "Arena" refers to the settings where the tools and artefacts are used, and the use in the different arenas may also be distributed from used much to used little. The property "Experiences" refers to what this work has led to. This property can be distributed on a scale ranging from good to poor or from very useful to not very useful.

In the 2008 edition of the book Corbin has simplified the paradigm model, placing causal circumstances, context and intervening circumstances under the umbrella term "circumstances". Under action and interaction strategies she

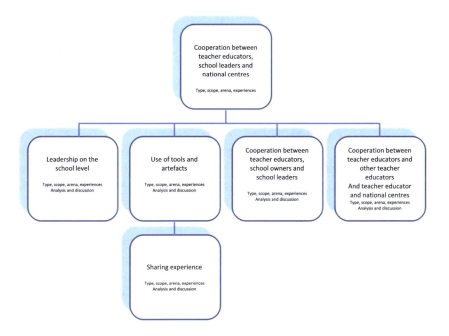

FIGURE 7.1 Overview of main categories, sub-categories and core categories

has also included emotions. This model still sees consequences as a separate factor. The paradigm model is used to identify the connection between context and process. In the 1990 and 1998 editions of the book Strauss and Corbin write that during the axial coding phase the researcher further structures the data material belonging to a category and develops the link between a category and its sub-category. These editions point out that the analytical process is not linear, but rather a process alternating between all the steps described in the analysis. This means that sub-categories can also be identified in the open coding phase, but that the material is structured and related to each other through the questions asked. These questions elicit which circumstances precede actions, interactions and emotions and which circumstances emerge along the way that also have consequences for these actions, interactions or emotions, and last, which consequences these actions, interactions and emotions have. In this way the paradigm model does not only make it possible to identify the relation between the context and the process, but also to structure the material within each individual category. The sub-categories within a category are also related to each other so that the researcher knows which sub-categories indicate circumstances, actions, interaction, emotions and consequences.

The "selective coding phase" (Strauss & Corbin, 1990, 1998) is where all the other categories are included to obtain answers to what it is all about and where the core category is developed. In our example the core category was "Cooperation", which includes all the actors and processes in the work. In this analytical phase questions are also asked on an on-going basis, and comparisons are made between categories. How does the cooperation between teacher educators and the other actors function if there is a specific form of school leadership (type), the leader has close contact with the teachers (scope) in different settings (arena), and this leads to experiences gained by the cooperation partners (good or poor). This may apply to one school. In another school the school leaders might lead the work in a different way, not having such up-close contact and where they only meet the teachers in plenary sessions. This also contributes to giving the participants experience, but probably other types of experience than what has been described above. Through constant comparison between the categories, their properties and how they are dimensioned, the researcher can point out similarities and dissimilarities in the material, which will form the basis for a thorough description and interpretation of the findings of the study. Based on the selective coding phase, the researcher can give a holistic answer to the main thesis.

Corbin and Strauss do not use the term selective coding in their 2008 edition but write about the core category and theory development. They maintain that the core category has analytical power and may explain or present what the research in is about in its entirety. This category is named using a more abstract concept than all the other categories. Corbin and Strauss (2008) explain that the analytical process should end in one core category so that only one theory is developed. If the analysis ends in two core categories, two theories must also be presented. They call this theory a substantive theory because it is not general. A general theory is not connected to a specific context but rather provides an abstract description, for example of teacher cooperation. A substantive theory presents teacher work in a specific context. The theory is thus contextual, developed within a specific setting within a certain period of time.

4.1   *Memos and Diagrams and Refining of Categories*
To aid in the analytical process to develop theory, the researcher can use memos and diagrams as analytical tools. Memos are spontaneous notes made on the researcher's analytical thinking. They may help the researcher to find an abstract concept and hence the name of the core category that may unite all the other categories. Diagrams, which are visual presentations of the analytical process as it progresses, can also help the researcher to name the core category.

If the researcher has a feeling that something is not right and some categories appear to be unfinished, he or she can check the internal consistency and logic by reviewing the memos and diagrams again. In the development of theory the goal is to arrive at a comprehensive theory, which means that the properties and dimensions of the category are identified and that variation is built into the theory. If the researcher finds that a category has not been adequately developed, he or she can return to the memos, diagrams and also the data material to examine whether something has been overlooked. When the researcher finds that the theory has reached the saturation point, meaning that each category has been presented in detail with regard to its properties, dimensions and variation, the refining of the categories can be concluded.

In the example above where school-based competence development is in focus, the researcher can use the categories and their dimensioned properties to explain why one setting with its actions and contexts contributes to better learning experiences than other settings with other actions and contexts. Therefore, this represents a theory that explains connections based on similarities and dissimilarities.

4.2   *Validation of the Theory*

When the theory outline is finished with all the categories built like a pyramid, with sub-categories, main categories and a core category, validation of the theory can begin. A theory represents an abstract reproduction of data. It is therefore important to examine how well the abstraction fits the data and whether something is found to be prominent in or even omitted from the proposed theory. To validate the theory outline, in addition to comparing the proposed theory with the data material, the researcher can ask the research participants to say whether they can recognise their situation in what has been written (Corbin & Strauss, 2008). This is also called member checking (Lincoln & Guba, 1985; Merriam, 1998; Savin-Baden & Major, 2013). The researcher can either tell the participants about his or her findings, or they can read a draft of the paper. The participants will obviously be unable to recognise every aspect of what has been written as the theory is a reduction of data based on several participants. In general, the research participants should be able to recognise their situation in what has been written. If it turns out that some of the data material does not fit, this often represents variations in the theory or alternative explanations. If the theory does not represent a variation, it is unlikely that it presents all the data in the material, as not everything in life can be so easily categorised (Corbin & Strauss, 2008). There will always be some variation in terms of the way leaders lead the development processes in school, and there will always be variation when it comes to teachers' cooperation. The cooperation between both leaders and teachers can also change and vary over time. This leads us to the processes.

5   Analysis of an On-Going Process

Corbin and Strauss (2008) define a process as on-going actions, interactions and emotions in response to a situation or problem, and most often with the purpose of reaching a goal or tackling a problem (pp. 96–97). In DWR, this refers to acting on an object, with the development question as the frame for actions and interactions. The context is important for how a process plays out. Various problems or situations may arise in a specific context and different goals may be set or different events may unfold. When contexts change, actions, interactions and emotions change. Which actions, interactions and emotional responses different contexts produce also depends on how the people in this context understand the situation. If a school leader opens for the sharing of experience between the teachers in a school, the way they cooperate and the knowledge they share collectively will probably develop. Developing good forms of cooperation can be a goal in this process. The new way in which the cooperation occurs and the knowledge is developed on the way to attaining the goal will in the next instance become part of the context for future emotional responses and for goal-directed actions and interactions. If the processes are to be analysed, the data must be collected over time in the research field, the dialogues aiming for development and the interviews and observations must grasp the changes in the context and in the goals and actions or interactions that are connected to these factors. I will return to the study of processes when I present the D-analysis method. If the researcher only collects data through interviews, he or she must also ask questions so that the history of the context, goals and actions, or interactions, are grasped in the interview. Thus development processes can also be described with the interview material as the point of departure.

6   Contextual Circumstances in the Analysis

In a situational or contingency matrix Corbin and Strauss (2008) present different layers of circumstances (context) that may impact the actions, interactions or emotions related to a phenomenon. In this matrix there are rings on rings which envelop each other with actions, interactions or emotions in the middle. The matrix presents circumstances from the micro to the macro level, such as from a teacher to the team level, to the organisational level, to the city government level and to the national and international levels. All these levels may be included in the analysis when they are useful and appropriate for understanding what is being studied and for presenting a comprehensive theory. When it comes to the above school-based competence development project, the catalyst for this was the poor results the pupils achieved in international tests. This means that a circumstance (causal relation in Strauss and Corbin's terms) explains why the national programme was implemented. *Rammeverk for skolebasert kompetanseutvikling* [General plan for school-based competence development], 2012/2017 (Norwegian Directorate for Education and Training, 2012) has served as the guideline for working with school-based competence development at the lower secondary level. The general plan informs about national frameworks, principles, roles and organisation of school-based competence development for the various programme areas. It establishes that since the work is school-based, it must be led by the principal. The school owner (the local government) is responsible for this work in the various municipalities. School-based competence development focuses on how everyone in a school should take part in developing the school's total knowledge, attitudes and skills in terms of learning, teaching and cooperation (Norwegian Directorate for Education and Training, 2012). The work will thus be important for each teacher individually and for the school as a whole. Based on this description, all circumstances, from the macro to the micro level, should be drawn on to analyse and understand the actions and interactions and the emotional responses in the school-based competence development.

7   Asking Questions and Making Comparisons

Asking questions and making comparisons are two important strategies in data analysis (Strauss & Corbin, 1990, 1998). Corbin and Strauss (2008) maintain that in addition to asking such questions as who, what, when, where, how and with what consequences, questions about time and space can also be posed. These may be questions focusing on frequency, duration, amount and time calculation, in addition to how much space the studied phenomenon has and how limited, open or closed it is. Using these questions the researcher may capture both properties and dimensions in the research work.

Corbin and Strauss (2008) find that the comparisons may be made in many ways. The first way is to compare events with other events or to compare statements with other statements to find similarities and dissimilarities. They refer to this as making "constant comparisons". These comparisons may help the researcher to separate a category or theme from another one and to identify properties and dimensions for each category. In this way similarities and dissimilarities in a category can be identified. For example, how close is the school leader to the teachers in the school-based competence development project, and in which arena does the leader interact with the teachers?

When the researcher makes comparisons in the data material using properties and dimensions, Corbin and Strauss (2008) call this making "theoretical comparisons". How does it impact the teachers' experiences (consequences) if the leader is close to them in different arenas (category 1 in Figure 7.2), while at the same time he or she facilitates for (circumstances) the teachers to observe, share experiences and reflect together (action/interaction) (category 2 in Figure 7.2)? What would such circumstances, actions and interactions, occurring either to a large or small extent, mean for the participants' learning outcome (consequences – described as experiences in Figure 7.2)? When the researcher conducts such comparisons, properties come to light that in turn may be used in the analysis of the data material. To help in these comparisons the researcher may use personal and professional experiences as well as theory. What do theories have to say about the importance of the leader in development processes in a school? What importance do various types of actions or interactions have in the development processes? The properties and dimensions that appear in both experiences and theory may help the researcher to examine the data material in the ongoing study. In this analysis, actions, interactions or emotions in the material are compared, but according to one's personal experiences or to theory. Focusing on properties and dimensions helps the researcher to move from a description to a more abstract explanation based on the comparison of properties and dimensions. This may help the researcher to explain what leadership in a school means rather than simply describing how it is carried out.

The properties and dimensions the researcher brings from the "outside" should not be used directly on the data material under study, but they may give the researcher ideas about what to look for, thus making the researcher sensitive in terms of what to look for, and whether there is something that has been overlooked.

8 Strategies in the Analytical Work

8.1 "Far-Out Comparisons"

At times similar settings and situations may be used to explore the data material, at other times completely different settings and situations may be compared (far-out comparisons). This strategy may be particularly useful when the analysis comes to a standstill and the researcher is unable to move on. As an example, Corbin and Strauss (2008) offer a comparison between a psychologist and a prostitute, both have clients and get paid for their services. This is also comparable to reflections that you might have when travelling abroad. When arriving in a country that is very different from your homeland, the experience may make you more aware of conditions in your own country.

The researcher also looks for actions, interactions and emotions in the analysis that stand out or do not fit into the pattern developed in the categorisation work. Examples which stand out from the complex understanding the researcher has developed in the analysis may contribute to an even more complete exploration of the dimensions of a category. Such examples make the explanations richer and show that everyone does not necessarily have the same understanding.

8.2   The "Flip-Flop" Strategy

The flip-flop strategy can be used when the researcher is blocked from seeing and understanding what the data material is revealing. This strategy literally involves turning things upside down (Corbin & Strauss, 2008). If the leader in a school leads development processes in a way that gives the impression that everything works, it may be difficult to see the large and small actions that actually make the work flow as well as it does. One way of proceeding then is to consider what a leader does in a school where the school-based competence development does not work so well. How does the leader lead in this school? How does he or she communicate with the teachers? How does he or she plan the work for the school-based competence development? How does the leader cooperate with the teachers in this work? In which arenas does the leader interact with the teachers in the school? What occurs during this interaction? How often are interaction meetings arranged? When the researchers consider this setting and what the leader does in it, it may open their eyes to what the leader does in the school where school-based competence development actually works.

8.3   Wave the Red Flag

When words such as "never" and "always" are used, or if the research participants state that "everybody knows that", you as a researcher, thinking in terms of properties and dimensions, should listen extra carefully. The researcher thinks about how statements may be distributed on a scale, and terms such as "always", "never", "everybody" and "not at all" represent only a single point on this scale. For the researcher, it is important to take nothing for granted and wave the red flag (Corbin & Strauss, 2008) when such terms are used. The researcher must ask what they mean; that is, what is meant by "never" or "always"? When is "never", and what circumstances are relevant then?

In conversations, the researcher must always remain aware of the words used and ask what the research participants mean when they say something that is unclear. The researcher can thus wave the red flag both in the on-going analysis when collecting the data and in the subsequent analysis.

9   Categories and Structure in a Written Presentation

Names of categories and sub-categories in the presentation of the findings form the structure of the presentation and hence the titles of chapters and their subsections. Names of categories can be theoretical concepts, even if the material has been analysed as inductively as possible. Statements by informants can be highlighted and can give names to both categories and chapter headings. Concepts named according to the research participants' words rather than being named by the researcher are called In-Vivo Codes (Strauss & Corbin, 1990, 1998; Corbin & Strauss, 2008). The researcher must be consistent in the use of such categories. If they are used for one category, they must also be used on any other categories. The words and statements used by the research participants that are rendered in the report should also give the reader a hint about the content of the category and thus the chapter.

In the analysis described above the structure or skeleton for the further analysis has been formed. As mentioned above I call this "descriptive analysis", which precisely deals with forming a structure for collected material (Postholm, 2010). In the written presentation of the chapters, examples from the category in question are highlighted and analysed using theory and earlier research. Dialogues between a researchers and teachers can for instance be examples presented with one category. The study is placed in a theoretical context and analysed. Theories can be both modified and developed in this analysis, and new theory can be developed. For this reason I call this process "theoretical analysis", fully aware that the descriptive analysis also has theory (Postholm, 2010). In this analytical process the researcher zooms in on each individual category which is an artificial division of the whole. However, this close analysis into each category facilitates for a comprehensive description and analysis of parts which together may supplement each other in the description of the whole. The core category includes all the other categories, and a presentation of this category could give full answers to research questions and the main thesis. I will deal with how findings can be presented in Chapter 9. In the following, I focus on how D-analysis can be conducted to understand development when focusing on language use.

ANALYSING THE DATA MATERIAL

10 Background for the Project Used as an Example for the Constant Comparative Analysis Method and D-Analysis

In a DWR project, I had several intervention sessions with 12 teachers working at the lower secondary level in a 1–10 grade school. We collaborated for two years, and during the first semester that could be understood as an own phase in the project – the start-up phase – the teachers were struggling to develop ownership of the project and how they should act on the object they had constructed together with me, the researcher. This study is also reported in an article titled "The Start-Up Phase in a Research and Development Work Project: A Foundation for Development in the journal Teaching and Teacher Education" (2008a).

During the first semester, we met for two hours every other week when all the teachers gathered at a scheduled meeting. The semester before the project started, we had constructed a development question in the frame of the current curriculum plan: How can various work methods with the focus on learning strategies contribute to each pupil's subject and social development? The teachers wanted to develop a more varied teaching method and present learning strategies for the pupils. The object was to support better subject and social development for the pupils. Although the teachers had taken part in constructing the development question, they did not seem to identify with the focus or the project, and they did not have any idea about how they could act on the object they had constructed. They needed to develop ownership in the project and determine how they could act on the object to develop their practice for the pupils' learning and development. I did not imagine beforehand that the teachers would need almost a whole semester to develop this ownership and to agree on what mediating artefact they should use to develop their practice towards the object.

During this first semester, I collected data by observing the teachers teaching and interviewing them in focus groups, both in class teams and in the team in which all the teachers were gathered. All the interviews were recorded and transcribed. Additionally, I recorded and transcribed the dialogues between teachers as well as between teachers and me, both in class teams and in the team in which all 12 teachers were gathered. The main category I developed when analysing the data material was "Developing ownership and a procedure in the start-up phase". Sub-categories were developed by asking when, why and under which circumstances this category surfaced and how and what it led to. I have already described that the teachers took part in a DWR project (when) and that they wanted to develop their teaching practice for the pupils' learning and development (why). In the following, I will go into the circumstances for the teachers' actions/interactions, how they acted/interacted and what it led to. I named the subcategories structuring the data connected to circumstances, how they acted/interacted and what they led to as follows: "From struggling with time to the use of time" and "A turning point to development". The subcategories forming sub-headings also signal movement or development. These categories are "member categories" (Middleton, 2010, p. 91), developed on the basis of the participants' utterances rather than decided a priori as factors in the activity system. The factors in the activity system could be used before the interventions to find contradictions or after the intervention to analyse the situation in practice and, eventually, detect new contradictions. In the following, I will present utterances and use D-analysis to understand how the teachers developed their ownership in the project and agreed on procedures (mediating artefact) for how to act on the object. However, before I go into the analyses, I will explain D-analysis and how they are generally conducted.

10.1 Conducting D-Analysis

Middleton (2010) describes D-analysis as analyses that find the form of communication of the participants taking part in DWR, with a primary focus on "what-it-is-to-learn" (p. 92). D-analysis therefore focus on communicative evidence of learning and on claims concerning knowledge states. A key point in the analyses is to detect distinctions in the dialogues that make contradictions in the practice visible. Middleton (2010) and his team developed a protocol to analyse communication in dialogues or discussions. The terms in this protocol were "deixis", "definition and delineation", "deliberation", "departure" and "development" (pp. 96–97); thus, in the name D-analysis, the "D" stands not only for the word discourse but also for all these terms. Below, I cite what these terms include.

Deixis: identify where there is some nomination or 'pointing' to a particular issue in terms of drawing attention to a distinction that is then worked up to make a difference in subsequent turns.

Definition and delineation: look for how that issue is elaborated in the uptake of others in terms of how the following are warranted and made relevant through: (i) qualifications identifying further distinctions; (ii) orderabilities in the organisation and delivery of past, present and future practice; (iii) expansive elaborations of the problems of practice.

Deliberation: identify how some working consensus on what is the case emerges in terms of evoking both particularities and generalities of marking distinctive features of past, present or future practice.

Departure: identify shifts toward qualititatively different position in practices in terms of the formulation of emergent distinctions.

Development: identify when participants specify new ways of working that provide the basis for becoming part of, or have become part of, what they take to warrant a significant reformulation of their practice (pp. 96–97).

Middleton (2010) and his team named the defined concepts for the D-analysis protocol that they used to identify strands of learning in terms of the emergence of distinctions that made a difference for the participants in their move towards multi-agency working. I will use the terms developed to analyse language use to identify the teachers' (working at the lower secondary level) development.

10.2   D-Analysis in a Concrete DWR Project

I present language use within the previously mentioned categories "From struggling with time to the use of time" and "A turning point to development".

10.2.1   From Struggling with Time to the Use of Time

When I asked the teachers if it is a good idea to share ideas about various work methods and learning strategies and talk about them in meetings with the various class teams and in the team gathering all the teachers, they answered that they already share ideas. One of them elaborated:

> We share experiences all the time. We do that all the time. And if we're frustrated about the pupils' behaviour we talk about it during class team meetings. And we suggest various solutions to each other.

Before this utterance, I asked the teachers whether it was a good idea to share ideas about work methods and learning strategies, as if these were issues they wanted to develop. I was thus 'pointing' to a particular issue by drawing attention to a distinction (deixis). The teacher quoted above presented a picture of how the situation was and has been when it comes to the sharing of ideas (definition and delineation). The teachers continued to explain that they did not talk about teaching sessions when they met. Rather, they discussed the planning of the teaching, the pupils, their behaviour and the relations between the pupils and between the pupils and the teachers. Moreover, they talked about creating a "bank" of teaching ideas:

> It has been, and continues to be the case that we all sit on each our turf and keep our plans to ourselves, instead of sharing ideas about teaching processes with each other. But we had to find time to do this. As it is now I think most of us think of it as another stress factor more than a teaching aid. And we have thousands of other things to do.

Here, the teacher is describing both the past and the present and indicating that the teachers have talked about creating a bank of ideas, thus delineating a future practice. The teacher saw the possibilities that the sharing of ideas could give them, but they experienced a contradiction: there was now time for sharing ideas. This was the necessary condition for the sharing of ideas.

During a meeting with all 12 teachers in the middle of October in the first semester, I stressed that sharing ideas about learning work is a good strategy. One intention of this meeting was to encourage the teachers to find a way to systematically reflect on their teaching together. They had already stated that they found it useful to talk about this when the project gave them a framework for doing so. It was also important to create continuity in these processes, making them part of the teachers' practice. In addition to arranging meetings to talk about reflection on teaching, I gave the teachers feedback on their teaching after observing them in the classroom (observation and feedback, as a new deixis). One of the teachers commented on this:

> I think it's good that we're allowed to talk together; that we get feedback on what we do from others. And, then we have the possibility to obtain information from the other teachers. We feel that we really need this, and that we focus on this and that we are reminded of what we do because teaching has become a habit.

Here, the teacher expressed her consensus (deliberation) that it is good that they are allowed to talk. She also took up the new issues that I had introduced (observing and giving feedback) and again expressed her consensus (deliberation) by using the collective "we". "We need it", she said, because when we are observed and get feedback we are reminded of what we do. They experienced this as a consequence, and they realised that they needed to conduct joint observations and reflections to develop their practice when it came to varied methods and learning strategies.

In the next meeting in late October, I suggested that the teachers make various work methods and learning strategies an agenda item for their class–team meeting every week and during every meeting when all the teachers gathered. In this meeting, they also made some deliberations regarding the sharing of ideas. One of the teachers commented: "We cannot manage every week, but perhaps every second week because we have so many pupils to talk about and the planning takes much of our time together". Another teacher agreed with her and elaborated:

> The discussions about the pupils can drain us of all the energy we have, and it can be good to work with things that raise our competence and

help us develop. I really hope that we can manage to make something like this. I really hope that we can manage to do something so concrete and useful.

This sparked a dialogue between some of the teachers:

Linda:	Yes, it's important to share ideas, but we never put aside time to do it.
Tor:	(overlapping). There's never time.
Researcher:	But if you think it's meaningful, you'll see that the time you use is meaningful.
Tor:	I agree; I don't disagree. But, it comes together with everything else.
	And, every time during the meetings we have to drop issues from the agenda list. And, we have to have time to plan.
Janne:	There is time, but it's a matter of what we use it for.
Tor:	Yes, we have to look at how we use the time we have.
Janne:	Things that are very useful ought to be given priority.
Tor:	All the time we have, new things to do, and we shouldn't hide the fact that when you came, it felt like yet another thing we had to do. What about the other things we have been instructed to do?
Ann:	But, sharing ideas is useful.

The teachers were still struggling with the time, and they elaborated on the problem of finding time in their practice (definition and delineation). However, they had started a discussion on how they could find time in the future (deliberation). It also seemed that all of them agreed that it was a good idea to share ideas (consensus). One teacher continued to talk about the issue of time in the same meeting:

> We should rather focus more on learning strategies during our meetings, we could see the pupils in the light of learning strategies. It's about our time, if we want to force ourselves to do it or if we are instructed to do it. We have to be more clever and not waste energy on cases which will bog us down. We have to be aware of what we are doing, and it is we that have to decide what to do. I think we just do more of the same, not doing any progress, but talking again and again about the same pupils.

The teacher described the situation as it has been and is (definition and delineation), and she said that they should use their time differently in the future.

She elaborated on the problems in their practice, noted that they just talked about the same pupils in their meetings and suggested what the future content in the meetings should be. She also said that it is the teachers who have to decide what to do (deixis), which reminded me, the researcher, that it was the practitioners' project and their practice that should be developed. My role was to provoke and sustain an expansive transformation process led and owned by the school leaders and teachers (Engeström & Sannino, 2010).

In the same meeting, the teachers suggested that they should undertake reflections in subject teams, a new arena for them to collaborate, and they wanted the team with lower secondary level teachers to meet more frequently. One teacher commented on this:

> We are a very creative group, and all of us certainly make a contribution, so it will take some time, and it's valuable time, and we have to let the headmaster know that this is time that is of great value to the school, so that we can have more meetings where we all meet to work on development. We have to have enough time for this project.

Here, the teacher used the word "we", signalling a consensus for future work (deliberation). This consensus was confirmed in an interview with the team leader November 1st, who indicated that the teachers saw the usefulness of sharing ideas: "I also think that the teachers also perceive this project as their own".

From this, I understood that I, the researcher, had to remain patiently in the background, curbing my enthusiasm and eagerness to accelerate development. That the teachers had developed ownership in the project really came to the forefront during a whole-day seminar at the end of November.

10.2.2   A Turning Point to Development

The team leader was chairing this whole-day seminar, and I was just observing, commenting and asking questions (I had taken up the deixis presented by the teacher, that is, the teacher had to decide what to do). During this seminar, the teachers decided that they wanted to not only share ideas but also observe each other in subject teams and reflect on the observed teaching in these subject teams afterwards (departure). The teachers had worked up what became a deixis during a meeting in the middle of October after I had observed and given feedback to them. The project was now moving forward, and the teachers had really taken control of it. It was rooted in the teachers' intentions, and they had developed ownership in it (led to development). In the next three semesters, the teachers observed and reflected together. As a result, they learned from each other and developed their teaching (Postholm, 2008b).

The teachers developed a sense of ownership of the project, but there were contradictions both in the team (primary contradictions) and between the subject, mediating artefacts and rules (secondary contradictions). The teachers in the team developed a consensus and ownership in the project as well as a procedure, including observation and reflection (mediating artefact), for how to act on the object; they found time in the timetable (rules). In CHAT, the view is that such contradictions are the starting point for change and development (Engeström & Sannino, 2010), as really became the result in the example project.

11   Concluding Reflection

In Chapter 2, I wrote that Helene and Erik could use the activity system as the analytical unit when carrying out DWR. This might seem confusing, as in the introduction to this chapter I state that the constant comparative analysis method can also be used together with D-analysis for such work. However, one approach does not exclude the other. The activity system is very useful when the situation is to be analysed both before and after a development project. After a development project, the system can be used to analyse whether old tensions and contradictions have been eliminated and whether the process has created new tensions and contradictions. If the goal for this work has been to promote teachers' learning, this system can be used to analyse the different factors in light of the researcher's focus – here teachers' learning. How has the community, and that includes the school leaders, supported teachers' learning? Which aids have been used in the learning process, and how have the teachers cooperated? This becomes a systemic analysis, where the individual parts of the system are analysed against each other. In the research, the researcher may also ask focused questions, such as 'How do the teachers perceive the support of the leaders in development activities?' To answer this question a phenomenological study can be conducted. Phenomenological analysis can be used to analyse collected materials in a phenomenological study to understand teachers' beliefs about their leaders' support" The constant comparative analysis method and the other analytical methods presented in Chapter 5 can be used as described when analysing materials within parts of the activity system. D-analysis can be used when trying to trace development in language use when individual parts of the system are analysed against each other, as in the example analysing the activity and focusing on the teacher team.

CHAPTER 8

Quality and Ethics

1   Introduction

Adequate research and ethical principles should go hand in hand in research processes, so I will examine quality and ethics in studies in this chapter. The quality of qualitative research refers both to how the findings presented should be useful in similar settings and situations and to having good quality in the research process itself. I will therefore focus on the research process and how the researcher can emphasise quality and ethical principles both in the process and in the research report so that it can be used as a thinking tool for others. First I will look at which knowledge qualitative studies end up providing.

2   Knowledge – Constructed and Intersubjective

The intention of research is to present knowledge, and for the researcher this also means to describe how the knowledge the research report provides has been constructed. The knowledge presented in the research report is the researcher's understanding developed in settings and situations that have been studied within the limits set by the frame of the research questions. This knowledge is also contextual because it is constructed according to the interaction between the researcher and the concrete setting where the research has been undertaken, and between the specific participants in the study. The research is thus not a search for universal knowledge, but rather the researcher will point to the diversity and context dependency of the knowledge. This knowledge is neither called subjective nor objective, but intersubjective. This is also what Kvale and Brinkmann (2015) call the knowledge that is created in a qualitative research interview. It is connected to people, time, location and situation.

Because knowledge is constructed in the interaction between the researcher and research participants, subjective relativism is avoided or that the knowledge that is the outcome of the research is experienced as true objective meaning. This knowledge is created through dialogic intersubjectivity, which can be a dialogue between several researchers, or between the researcher and research participants (Kvale & Brinkmann, 2015). The qualitative researcher also strives to be sensitive to his or her own prejudices and subjectivity. This is referred to as being reflexive in the research process (Glesne, 2011; Kvale &

Brinkmann, 2015; Lincoln & Guba, 2000). This means trying to be aware of how a researcher might influence the research process and the resultant findings. According to Heshusius (1994), however, the researcher can never be completely objective when it comes to his or her own subjectivity, but the point is that the researcher must try to be aware of this so it can be presented as part of the context in which the findings can be understood (Merriam, 2002).

To be aware of his or her own subjectivity, the researcher could write notes regularly in a logbook about his or her own role. When returning to the notes, the researcher could arrive at a meta-view of this own role and how observations and the content of interviews are perceived and understood according to the researcher's own position. In the research process researchers might be led to collect data material that supports their own assumptions and thus hear and see what they want to find. By writing in the logbook before and after the data collection, researchers can address these anticipated perceptions and reflect on them (Glesne, 2011). The researcher is in dialogue with him- or herself in this logbook. Researchers can also enter into dialogue with other researchers or research participants in the research process to be aware of how they understand, and in this dialogue they can develop their own understanding so it become more nuanced. This does not mean that this understanding becomes true, but thoughts and understandings can be developed in dialogue with others (Vygotsky, 2000). In qualitative research and in DWR the researcher can never be neutral. The principle of objectivity is not a desirable principle in qualitative research.

3   Concepts Representing Quality

Various concepts are used about the credibility of studies. In addition to objectivity which I dealt with in the section above, we find reliability and validity. These concepts refer to how the researcher can assure the quality of the study. Some researchers choose to use other terms than reliability and validity because they feel these two terms belong in the quantitative research tradition (Kvale & Brinkmann, 2015). Guba (1981) has replaced these concepts, which he believes have a positivist origin, with: credibility instead of internal validity, transferability instead of external validity, dependability instead of reliability and confirmability instead of objectivity. All these concepts can act as criteria for a study's credibility. If the researcher considers all these factors and shows how the research process was carried out to ensure quality in the study, the study will be more credible. Before elaborating on Guba's concept, I will examine the reliability and validity concepts in more detail.

3.1 Reliability and Validity

Reliability refers to the consistency of the research results and whether they can be reproduced at other times by other researchers (Kvale & Brinkmann, 2015). It can, in my opinion, be difficult to replicate a qualitative study because the interaction between the researcher and the research field and the participants in the study will be different, because different researchers will use their subjective individual theory (see Chapter 3) in the research and because all people are always in development, including researchers and research participants. It is also important to ask what the intention is in repeating a study. Will the study be truer if the findings in the replicated study are the same, and is such thinking controlled by the existence of one truth? The answer to the first part of this two-fold question is no, and to the second part it is an unequivocal yes. I have touched on how findings in a study represent contextual knowledge, and that the researcher's subjectivity must be presented as part of the context the findings are to be understood in. Bearing this in mind, reproducing a study has no impact on its trustworthiness.

Validity refers to whether a method is suitable for studying what is to be examined. Does the study find the answer to what is being asked, or in Kerlinger's (1979) words: "Are you measuring what you think you are measuring" (p. 138)? Measurement implies a result given as a number, and this means that according to this definition of quality, a qualitative study will not have validity. As I said in Chapter 2, research questions can be developed during the research process. This applies in particular to DWR where the development processes and thus the progress of the work are not known in advance.

In a qualitative study where the researcher's mission is to conduct research but not support development at the same time the research can also take a slightly different direction than the researcher had envisioned originally, bearing in mind that he or she is abductive (Alvesson & Sköldberg, 2009) in the research process. This may mean that in the end the main research question has to be modified and refined to frame the study findings (see Chapter 3). In both these cases the process is what determines which data material will be included in the presentation of the study and which main research question it will end up with. Therefore there is little point in the qualitative study having a locked main research question when starting up the work to assess how valid the findings are. The researcher should, however, describe how the main research question and the sub-questions were developed during the research process. Wolcott (1994) argues that the concept of understanding can replace the validity concept. The researcher should therefore describe how he or she arrived at this understanding, thus making the research process transparent, and should also describe how the researcher's on-going analysis contributed to his or her emerging understanding.

3.2 Credibility, Reliability, Confirmability and Transferability

As described above, the concepts of credibility, reliability confirmability and transferability all refer to how to give a study trustworthiness. According to Lincoln and Guba (1985) activities in the research field that may improve "credibility" (or trustworthiness) include the following:

- prolonged engagement in the research field
- persistent observation
- dialogue with other researchers
- analysis of cases/events that indicate the opposite of the main finding
- referential accuracy
- triangulation (data sources, several methods and researchers)
- member checking (both in the research process and at the end). (p. 328)

I will first briefly comment on some of the points before discussing triangulation and member checking in more detail. Prolonged engagement in the research field means a long stay in relation to the focus of the researcher in his or her research. A Master's degree study should not have too wide a main research question so the researcher can examine in depth the theme in focus without spending too much time on data collection. A Master's degree course obviously has a limited time perspective. Moreover, according to Lincoln and Guba (1985) it is necessary to carry out persistent observations to achieve understanding, but I would also add that it is necessary to talk with the participants to grasp the meaning behind the observed actions (cf. what I said in Chapter 6 about data collection and what is sufficient information in a study within a constructivist paradigm). I have already mentioned how the researcher can be in dialogue with others to elaborate on his or her understanding of the theme being studied. Moreover, as Lincoln and Guba (1985) state, an analysis of incidents or actions which show the opposite of the main findings helps to highlight the complexity of the theme being studied. As part of the researcher's scientific accuracy it is important that the references are accurate, in other words, pointing out clearly what are your own words and what are the words of others whom you refer to. Below I will examine triangulation and member checking in more detail as these are two key methods for assuring the quality of a study.

When the researcher refers to several sources we call this triangulation. Using many forms of data collection is the most common way of triangulating

(Creswell, 2013), as is the use of many data sources, such as leaders, teachers, pupils and parents, as well as additional researchers and different theoretical perspectives (Creswell, 2013; Glesne, 2011; Stake, 1995). The term triangulation used to describe a method for assuring the quality of a study is a metaphor derived from navigating at sea (Stake, 1995). Skippers and fishermen needing to find their position, route or a fertile fishing ground would first find their position based on two different axes and would use a third point or more axes to confirm that they were in the correct position. When the third axis (or axes) intersected the crossing point of the other two axes, they were in the correct position to sail or to land a good catch.

Triangulation can remind one of a similar procedure that has the intention of describing reality as it is, and that it therefore has a positivist point of departure. In a constructivist paradigm triangulation may be seen as a procedure for grasping reality there and then as the research project is in progress, knowing very well that the setting and the people, including the researcher, are constantly changing and developing (cf. my comment relating to reliability). In the positivist stance the researcher must describe things as they really are, while in the interpretative perspective the researcher would rather understand things according to the possible sources and perspectives he or she starts with. Perhaps the researcher interprets incorrectly or fails to see the nuances in the data material. Then other perspectives, emerging from the material, different theoretical perspectives or in conversation with other researchers, may help the researcher to see his or her own limitations and possibly which version is the most likely. According to Gibbs (2015) it can also be beneficial for the researcher to discover that what a research participant has said in observations and interviews is inconsistent with what this participant actually does. The point is not to demonstrate that the research participant is lying or wrong, but to point out additional dimensions in the social reality which reveal that people do not always act consistently. According to Gibbs inconsequence or contradictions can help to unmask the complexity of a situation.

Member checking refers to how the researcher checks the data material, analytical categories, interpretations and conclusions with those who have participated in the research (Lincoln & Guba, 1985; Merriam, 1998; Savin-Baden & Major, 2013). In the course of a DWR project the research participants' practices are reflected back to them through the collected material and the researcher's analyses of this material (Cole & Engeström, 2007). In conversations with the research participant the researcher also receives feedback on an ongoing basis about how he or she understands the participants' situation. The continuous feedback the researcher receives can be understood as member checking (Lincoln & Guba, 1985; Merriam, 1998; Savin-Baden & Major, 2013) of the material collected during the entire project period, and the credibility of the research will therefore be strengthened. Knowledge is both generated and tested in practice (Greenwood & Lewin, 2007).

When researchers want feedback on a written report text, both in the context of research and DWR, they can, for example, ask the participants to read parts of a description of the setting and the situations studied, without any theoretical framework and the researcher's analyses. Such feedback or member checking can give the researcher an answer to the question Stake (1995) asks: "Do we have it right?" (p. 107). The researcher will then receive feedback on whether the description of the school situation is right, and the research participants can see their statements as part of the description, and might want to offer corrections on what they have stated without necessarily changing the content. When speech is transferred to written text, the statements could be seen as clumsy, and the research participants might at times want to refine what they have said. The researcher might also want to receive feedback on the entire text, analytical categories, interpretations and conclusions as Lincoln and Guba (1985) suggest, but consideration should be given to how much work this entails for the research participants, and whether they have the opportunity and time to read analyses and interpretations to give the researcher feedback. While the participant could be given access to the entire research text, the researcher should keep in mind what he or she wants feedback on. It is, however, a good ethical principle that the research participants who have participated in the research that the text is based on are the first readers of this text.

When it comes to promoting "reliability", according to Lincoln and Guba (1985), this refers to the researcher being like an auditor who must show how the accounts have been kept, so that the research process can be reviewed and approved. An example of having a transparent research process is shown in Appendix 3 where we see how the researcher has collected data and what the content of the different sources is at specific periods of time. If the researcher has studied a planning document before a class, observed the class and interviewed the observed teacher after the class, this can be entered as a reference in the text as follows: (plandoc 19/03/2018, obsnot, 20/03/2018, intteacher 20/03/2018). If the researcher lists in an attachment what the content of the planning document (plandoc) is, sums up the content of the observation (obsnot) and briefly describes the content of the interview with the teacher (intteacher), the reader of the paper can go back and forth like an auditor to check if everything agrees and the sources support each other. To facilitate the researcher's work, abbreviations can be used with dates that refer to the data material and a list of these abbreviations can be provided. References to the data material can then be made in much the same way as when the researcher refers to the texts of other researchers in his or her own text.

"Confirmability" refers to the fact that the researcher must ensure that there is a foundation for the analyses and interpretations in the description of the data material, and that there is cohesion between the descriptions, analyses and interpretations that are made. Lincoln and Guba (1985) label this concept confirmability. When the researcher refers to the data material in the text, as described above, he or she shows that the data material forms the foundation for the findings that are presented. Making the research craft transparent and providing a description of how the categories have emerged out of the research process, based on memos when the constant comparative analysis method is used (see Chapter 7), is another way of showing that the descriptions, analyses and interpretations are based on the data material.

To strengthen the credibility of the presented findings with experts and intended readers, it is important that the researcher writes in such a way that the reader feels invited into the research process, or into both the development processes and the research if we are referring to a DWR project. This improves the transferability of the study to other similar settings and situations. The researcher needs to describe the research and the DWR project, thus making the work transparent. The development questions and/or the research focus through one or more research questions frame the practice so that parts of it may be zoomed in on or developed if that is also an intention of the work and has been researched. The presented knowledge is a substantive theory or theories relating to a specific part or parts of a complex holistic reality which plays out in practice (Postholm, 2010, see Chapter 3). The role of the theory is to describe and explain what has taken place and, moreover, to point out future opportunities for development and research. The theory can thus both support and elaborate on findings in similar studies, and it can also contribute new knowledge.

According to Geertz (1973) it is necessary to present "thick descriptions" which deal with both actions and meanings, and also the context for these actions and meanings, to the reader, who should also feel invited into the researcher's concrete research situation and the perspectives of the participants. This is supported by Lincoln and Guba (1985). From reading the research text, the reader can also develop his or her understanding of the research and the research findings presented, and perhaps also apply this as a naturalistic generalisation (Stake & Trumbull, 1982). Such a generalisation implies that the reader perceives what he or she is reading as parallel experiences and adapts and transfers these to his or her own setting ("transferability"). Thus the research text will be useful and relevant for the reader because it can function as a thinking tool (Gudmundsdottir, 2001) and a development tool for the reader's own practice.

CHAT focuses on analyses of practice in both a historic and contemporary perspective before any new solutions are addressed (Engeström, 1987, 1999, 2001; Virkkunen & Newnham, 2013). In these phases the researcher collects data material as the basis for development. The data material collected can also be used for research purposes. In this way, in his or her role as a supporting resource person in development processes and as a researcher on them, the researcher contributes to making the data material and the analyses support the development while the work is being performed in the schools, and also enabling it to be presented in research texts which others in similar settings can use as a thinking tool to develop their own practice (Gudmundsdottir, 2001). DWR therefore will have definite utility value. It will be useful for those who are in the practice that is being developed and researched, and it can also be useful for others in similar settings and situations. The new knowledge is thus very relevant for the practice.

Wardekker (2000) writes that school researchers often have experience from school. He therefore asks whether it is ethically appropriate that researchers doing research in what is for them a familiar context should not also contribute to supportive development while the research is on-going. In research I conducted on project work, the teachers asked whether I could also offer input on how they could carry out the project. The teachers knew that I had written a book about project work, and therefore they rightly questioned why my role did not also include intervening in the processes. We then turn our focus to ethical principles.

4   Ethical Principles in Research

An all-inclusive ethical principle in research is that the researcher's responsibility must first be presented to the research participants, then in relation to the study and finally in relation to the researcher personally (Fontana & Frey, 2000). If, for example, a researcher observes that a teacher does not address bullying in a class, which the teacher apparently also observes, the researcher should raise this with the teacher, even if this may entail the risk of the research project being stopped. Ethical principles in research and DWR activities should be maintained prior to starting the research, during the research process and in the text produced on the basis of the research.

Chapter 4 presented a suggestion for the content in a letter sent to schools that welcome or have been selected for research. This letter makes the practical implications clear, explains the role of the researcher and what he or she wants to do with the findings, states why this venue for research has been chosen and why certain people have been selected, and also informs about what they will get in return for their participation. This type of letter to research participants will also normally guarantee "anonymity" by stating that the participants will be given "pseudonyms" in all written texts, both in the transcriptions and the final report text, and that information will be dealt with "in confidence" (Glesne, 2011; Kvale & Brinkmann, 2015; Rubin & Rubin, 2005; Stake, 1995). It is also common to inform that data collection and data processing will follow and comply with research ethics principles. While this is an information letter, part of the intention is also to build a trusting relationship with the research participants. It is therefore also important for the researcher to deliver on the promises made before the research was started so that this trust can be maintained and perhaps even developed during the research process. In a DWR project it will be particularly important to build trust based on the researcher's professional, emotional and social competence, which I discussed in Chapter 4 in connection with roles and access to the research field.

When the information is given before the research and DWR begins, the research participants will know what they have agreed to. When they agree to participate they will have given their "informed consent" (Bogdan & Biklen, 2007; Glesne, 2011; Kvale & Brinkmann, 2015; Moustakas, 1994). But there may be cases where the researcher is unable to disclose all the information as it may have an effect on the actions and interactions that play out, thus influencing the research. If the researcher wants to conduct a micro-ethnographic study of a learning environment in a class where the researcher knows bullying takes place and he or she wants to study this, little bullying will be in evidence if the researcher states that that particular problem is the point of the study. In such a case it is important to be sufficiently open, but not so precise that it will undermine the research. The researcher could state that the aim is to study group processes in the class or the teacher's classroom management of the learning activity.

After the research process itself is over and the research text has been written, it is a good ethical principle to let the research participants be the first readers of the report text, as I have touched upon earlier. The researcher should also remove all information in the text that could be detrimental for the participants (Moustakas, 1994, Rubin & Rubin, 2005). It is not ethically defensible to place research participants who have been willing to spend their time on the research in a bad light so that it could be unfavourable (Rubin & Rubin, 2005). This might mean that the researcher has to withhold information or findings that are relevant to the research because presenting these findings would be unethical. This is consistent with Fontana and Frey's (2000) ethical principle that says the researcher's responsibility to the research participant must override the study's goals.

5 Quality and Ethics – A Summary

I will here summarise some key points relating to quality and ethics in research by presenting Merriam's points on ethics, which have been divided into four sections: problem, methods, findings and discussion. Below I use this division in the presentation of the points.

Problem
1. Is the problem appropriate for qualitative inquiry? Is the question one of meaning, understanding or process?
2. Is the problem clearly stated?
3. Is the problem situated in the theory? That is, is the theory used to put the problem in context?
4. Is the relationship of the problem to previous research made clear?
5. Is the researcher's perspective and relationship to the problem discussed? Are assumptions and biases revealed?
6. Is a convincing argument explicitly or implicitly made for the importance or significance of the research? Do we know how it will contribute to the knowledge base and practice?

Methods
1. Has the particular qualitative research design been identified and described (basic interpretive, grounded theory, phenomenology, ethnography and so on)?
2. Has the sample selection been described including rationale for criteria used in the selections?
3. Are data collection strategies described and do they fit the problem being investigated and the approach that has been presented?
4. How has the data material been managed and analysed?
5. What strategies were used to ensure validity and reliability?
6. What ethical considerations are discussed?

Findings
1. Have the participants in the study been described? (This could also be put under methods.)
2. Are the findings clearly organised and easy to follow?

3. Are the findings directly responsive to the problem examined in the study? That is, do they "answer" the research question(s) raised by the study?
4. Does the data material presented in support of the findings (quotations from interviews, incidents from field notes, material from documents and so on) provide adequate and convincing evidence for the findings?

Discussion
1. Are the findings "positioned" and discussed in terms of the theory and previous research?
2. Are the study's insights and contributions to the larger body of knowledge clearly stated and discussed?
3. Are the implications for practice discussed?
4. Do the implications the study points out follow from the data?
5. Are there suggestions for future research?
(Merriam, 2002, p. 23)

CHAPTER 9

Writing up the Research Project

1   Introduction

This chapter deals with how the research process and research findings can be presented in a written text. I use the master's thesis as an example, as Erik is studying for a master's degree. However, the presentation can be useful for research at all levels, also for teacher educators/researchers who supervise student teachers or conduct research or collaborate in DWR in school. First, I will examine the researcher's position and the recipients of the study. Then I will describe what can be presented in the introduction to a Master's thesis. This will be followed by a look at thick and thin descriptions, and after this I will present how to structure the content of the entire thesis. In this context I will point out that in DWR the researcher must make a distinction between what is development and what is research. Descriptions are a key part of qualitative research so in one section below I will look into how description can be the springboard for further analysis. Descriptions also feature the voices of the participants through the use of extracted quotations. I will also show how quotations can be placed in the text before ending the chapter with a description of how the researcher can establish a connecting theme in the Master's thesis.

2   The Thesis and the Researcher's Position

When sitting down to write the thesis the first step is to assemble all the parts into a coherent whole. Strauss and Corbin describe this step (1990) with a metaphor: this is the architecture of the study, comparing the thesis to a house where the reader can visit each room, or each chapter, to learn about the whole house, or the content of the thesis. When structuring the thesis and presenting the content the researcher is the master builder. Earlier when there was a focus on an objective presentation, the researcher would use a third-person omniscient voice (Tierney, 1997). When acknowledging that the researcher is bringing his or her subjectivity into the research the first-person perspective "I" is allowed in the research text (Wolf, 1992). This means that Helene, Erik, Leander and Leona can use the personal pronoun "I" when they write. Creswell (2013) claims that the researcher is rather more self-revealing today than only a few years ago, and that it is no longer acceptable for the qualitative researcher to present him- or herself as an omniscient and distanced writer. According to Richardsen and St. Pierre (2005), "researchers do not have to try to play God, writing as disembodied omniscient narrators claiming universal and atemporal general knowledge" (p. 961). Richardson (1994) talks about qualitative reports as texts with a sub-text which situates or positions it historically within a specified place at a defined point in time. This text, according to Gilgun (2005), can be understood as a representation of interactions between the researchers and research participants where all the voices should be heard. It is not a given that the reader will understand the text in the same way as the researcher who wrote it because a dialogue will arise between the written text and the reader where the reader's subjectivity comes into play. Moreover, language has its limitations, and according to van Manen (2016), qualitative researchers realise that it is impossible to write in such a way that the text resulting from the research will be understood in the same way by all.

In Chapter 8 I addressed the concept of reflexivity, which means that the researcher is sensitive to the presence of his or her own prejudices and subjectivity (Glesne, 2011; Kvale & Brinkmann, 2015; Lincoln & Guba, 2000). The researcher's subjectivity and its importance should also be pointed out in the research text. First the researcher in the introduction to the thesis can describe his or her experiences of the issues being studied. This could be through employment, education or family life. Second, the researcher should also discuss how these previous experiences might have influenced the analyses and the findings. The researcher should consider how to present this discussion. It could be written in the methods section in connection with the researcher role, or as Stake (1995) proposes, as a vignette at the end of the thesis.

3   The Recipients of the Thesis

When the researcher writes it will be easier to find the right phrases if the recipients or potential readers of the text are known. When a Master's degree student is writing the thesis, he or she may feel that the thesis is being written for people with the same competence. This means that method theory and other relevant theories, from theoretical models to substantive theory, can be included in the text. Once the thesis has been submitted and the examination has been passed, the findings may also be made available to a more general readership in an article in such media as popular science magazines or newspapers. The text will then have a narrower scope, and the findings can be presented without the comprehensive theoretical framework that is in the original thesis. Such variation in presentation is supported by Giorgi (1985), who maintains that the presentation of findings depends on the readers the researcher wants to communicate with.

4 The Introduction in the Thesis

The introduction will tell the readers what the thesis is about, its relevance, the aim of the study and why it is important. This is also where the main research question and the sub-questions will be presented, showing how they were developed during the research process. One of the first things the introduction should do is place the themes raised in the study in a social and theoretical context to show the thesis's relevance. Here white papers and other national governance documents can be referred to. The theoretical framework of the study can be briefly presented along with a short overview of earlier research in the field. This introductory text can then end with the main research question for the study, where the research questions are also presented. After this, the researcher can give the rationale for the aim of the research and why it is important. The aim of the study can be formulated as follows:

> The aim of this _____ (case, ethnographic phenomenological) study has been to _____ (understand, describe, develop, discover) the _____ (main phenomenon/theme of the study) for _____ (the participants) at _____ (the site). At this stage in the research text, the (main phenomenon/theme) will be generally defined as _____ (a general definition of the main concept). (Creswell, 2013, p. 135)

If school-based competence development is the phenomenon/theme that is to be studied, a general definition can be:

> School-based development means that the school, including school leaders and the entire staff, is undergoing a workplace development process. The aim is to develop the school's collective knowledge, attitudes and skills when it comes to learning, teaching and collaboration. (Directorate for Education and Training 2012, p. 5; my translation)

After the aim of the study has been given a rationale, the researcher can argue as to why the research is important. As a final paragraph in the introduction the researcher could write a meta-text or guide informing the reader about the further structure of the thesis and briefly about the content of the subsequent chapters.

4.1 Formulation of the Main Research Question, Aim and Importance of the Studies

Formulation of the main research question or the problem will include the concept that refers to the theme of the study. Based on the theme presented above this will be school-based competence development. Anyone unaccustomed to producing research texts may find it difficult to express that the study is about a problem, finding this to be a misleading term. In research the intention of the problem for research is to ensure that there is a logical explanation or reason to explain why there is a need to study a particular theme or problem (Creswell, 2013). The term "problem" is therefore connected to method and not to a mundane challenge.

In a study of the Norwegian national programme *Ungdomstrinn i utvikling* (UiU – Lower secondary stage in development) lasting four years and five months (from the autumn of 2013 and until the end of 2017), where school-based competence development was a strategy for satisfying the programme goals,[1] the following main research question and sub-questions were the basis for the research carried out by a group of researchers (Postholm et al., 2018):

Main Research Question
– What importance has UiU had for development on different levels in school and education?

Sub-Questions
– What have the participants in UiU learnt by taking part in the programme?
– How have the various participants learnt by taking part in the UiU programme?
– How is what they have learnt expressed in school and in the participants' practices? (p. 94)

In this study university and college sector staff were supporting resource persons in all participating lower secondary schools and schools with lower secondary stages in Norway. The aim of the study was to illuminate the content of the programme, analyse its importance and find implications for the framework and organisation of future development projects. Thus this research was important for decisions on how to develop and organise future work in schools.

In other studies the researcher might have focused on the teacher's role as a leader in the classroom when it comes to motivating the pupils for learning. The aim of the study could then be to describe activities the teacher introduces to motivate the pupils so that the text could serve as a thinking tool for others. Based on the findings, the researcher could then also point out implications for the teacher role. Another study could have focused attention on the way teachers talk when reflecting on their mutually observed teaching. The aim of the study could then be to describe a teacher team which communicates in such a way that teachers learn together. But this requires that the researcher has a focus that can serve this aim. Conversation analysis and D-analyses would reveal how they talk, and the text could then function as inspiration for others who are cooperating in this area.

If he researchers are clear right from the start about what the study is about and why it is important, it can be easier to point out the common thread in the study, from start to finish, where the implications for the study are to be presented. Having a clear aim for the study will also have an effect on the choice of the sample as it must serve the purpose of the study, what is called an appropriate sample (see also about appropriate sample in Chapter 5).

The researcher also uses concepts in the research questions to code the type of study that is to be carried out, whether it is qualitative and also which approach is to be used (Creswell, 2013, Postholm, 2010). If the researcher is planning to conduct a phenomenological study the word "experience" will often be part of the main research question. Other coded cues for the reader are through the use of words in the main research question, with concepts such as learning environment (micro ethnography), an incident, activity or programme (case study), curriculum (text analysis) or conversation (conversation analysis). The cue will be elaborated on when the researcher explains the aim of the study.

The research questions presented above (Postholm et al., 2018), which start with "what" and "how", point out that the responses may be presented as a descriptive text offering the participant's perspective. It can also be assumed that the researcher obtains answers to these questions through interviews. The third research question refers to how the learning is expressed and suggests that the researcher should also observe the practice. If the question had asked how the participants have experienced or are experiencing how learning is expressed in school and in the their practice, interviews could also have been a sufficient data collection strategy for answering this question. These answers will in turn help to answer the main research question and explain the importance of UiU for development on different levels in school and education.

5   Thick and Thin Descriptions

Geertz (1973) developed the idea of thick and thin descriptions in his review of the collected articles of Gilbert Ryle. Ryle asks the reader to think about two boys who quickly wink their right eye. For one of them this is a reflex action, for the other a conspiratorial signal to a friend. According to Ryle, as described earlier, one of the boys is performing one single action, winking an eye, while the other is doing two things, both winking and giving a sign. Ryle sees winking on purpose when there is a public code as being both a sign and part of the culture. If a writer describing this scenario states that a boy winks his eye, this is a "thin description". When this action is a sign, the action has been ascribed meaning which may be understood in the setting it was performed in. If the researcher is to be able to grasp and understand this difference, according to Geertz (1973), he or she needs background information. The action must be understood in its context. This means that the situation as it is and as it was in the setting that is being studied must be described. Culture refers to the different ways in which groups act and which convictions they have for these actions (Wolcott, 2008). In the second point in the expansive learning cycle the historic and current situations are precisely what are in focus (see Chapter 2). To obtain an understanding of these two situations we use both observations and interviews. The researcher can thus develop an understanding of the culture and write a "thick description", which will be a construction of understanding based on the collected material. The thick description thus represents the researcher's understanding of the situation and the actions studied.

According to Geertz (1973) ethnography provides thick descriptions. Wolcott (2008) also sees the importance of descriptions in ethnographic studies, maintaining that descriptions are "the bedrock" (p. 53) of such studies. He points out that this applies to all qualitative studies where the intention is to present the participant perspective.

6   How to Structure the Text

Following the introduction in a Master's thesis it is common to present the theoretical foundation that frames the study. These will be theoretical models, such as Dewey's pragmatism, Vygotsky's socio-cultural studies or CHAT (see Chapter 2 and 3). The theory section will introduce important concepts (intermediate theories) in the thesis. Previous research in the field can then be presented after the theory section or this research may be presented together with the overarching theory if the main chapter heading is "Theory and related research". After presenting the theory and related research, the researcher should describe the setting where the research has taken place. This description will provide contextual information that will lead to understanding of the findings. As part of the contextual information, Postholm (2018b) described a school as follows in connection with the study of the UiU programme:

> School A1 is a lower secondary school in a rural town. The school has 156 pupils, 17 teachers and two leaders, a principal and vice-principal. The school has two parallel classes in Years 8 and 9, and three parallel classes in Year 10. The school is working on classroom management and reading in the UiU programme, in both the pilot programme and group 1. After the participation in the programme came to an end, in the autumn of 2015 the teachers started working with assessment for learning (AfL), and they had started to use the open AfL web course and MOOC: (massive open online course) prepared by Lillehammer University College. (p. 323)

This was a research project where the researcher had not participated in the development processes. If the description is not too detailed, it can be included in the introduction of the methods chapter. If the researcher is conducting a DWR project, which means researching development that the researcher also supports, it will be important to separate the description of the development project from the research process, even if these processes merge when the DWR project is carried out. In a DWR project the contextual information for the research and the findings presented will most likely be more comprehensive than in a research project as the researcher both supports and undertakes research on the development processes, which then might need to be in a separate chapter. The models presented in Chapter 2 can be used to describe the development work. The activity system can be used to describe the tensions and contradictions in and between factors as the starting point for development. Moreover, the expansive learning circle or the primary or secondary circle in the R&D model can be used to describe how development was planned and carried out. Finally, the action learning circle can be used to explain how the described measures were tested in different settings and situations, such as the teaching in the classroom or cooperation between teachers in the team room.

In the methods section the researcher first describe qualitative method in general, before describing the specific approach used. Thereafter the choice of research venue and research participants and how the researcher gained access to the field can be described. Appendix 1 provides a sample letter of consent that can be used in this context. Following this the research process and how the researcher has collected the data material can be described before the researcher elaborates on how the material was analysed. This analysis can be shown as in Figure 7.2 in Chapter 7. After this, the researcher role can be presented.

The description of the researcher role will depend on whether the researcher has carried out a research project or a DWR project. In both cases the description should be followed by a self-analysis of the role the researcher has had during the work. However, the description and analysis should be more detailed if the researcher has carried out DWR, as in this case the researcher will have two roles. A journal or logbook can be an important tool for the researcher during the process to note down and remember perceptions and experiences that arise during the work. These notes will, as described earlier, also be useful when the researcher will be describing and analysing his or her own role in the work. In connection with the description of this role, the researcher's own subjectivity can also be pointed out along with a description of how assumptions and personal experiences and perception might have influenced the processes and findings in the study. After dealing with the researcher role, a natural next move would be to discuss quality-assurance of the study, as well as ethical principles and how they have been complied with in the study, as the researcher's role impacts both. When describing the quality of the study it is important to keep Merriam's (2002) points in mind and to discuss the ones that are relevant for the study in question. This also applies to the ethical principles (see Chapter 8).

The findings from the study are presented after the methods section. Above I referred to Wolcott (2008) who writes that the description is the bedrock of qualitative studies. A description based on collected material can therefore be presented before an analysis and interpretation. This description will become part of the thick description together with the context which has already been presented, and which the researcher uses as the point of departure for analysis and interpretation. According to Wolcott (2001) it is important to focus on the description until the researcher has prepared a solid basis for the analyses. This description can start with the divisions into topics of the settings and situations that have been studied. These descriptions can be called "descriptive categories". According to Wolcott (2008) the analyses should be separated from the interpretation and in the analysis the researcher will follow familiar procedures when presenting facts, figures and findings. Interpretation, according to Wolcott, is what we as researchers understand according to the data and the analyses. These are interpretations that are based on the data material and analyses of it but are not overwhelmed by these in direct dialogue with others.

Initially the researcher conducts a descriptive analysis (Postholm, 2010) which serves as the skeleton or scaffolding for the further analysis (Charmaz, 2014). I have described constant comparative analysis as one method that can be used in all qualitative approaches (see Chapter 7). "Analytical categories" are developed in the descriptive analysis and they can form the structure for the presentation of the findings (see Figure 7.2 in Chapter 7). For each category that represents a chapter, substantive theory and relevant research can be referred to before presenting the data material, which is then analysed according to the relevant theory and the research findings. The analysis and findings can be supported by previous research, can correct this or can also present new findings.

In connection with the main categories "From struggling with time to the use of time" and "A turning point to development" presented in chapter 7, D-analyses were used to understand development. D-analyses could also have been used in connection with the main category "Sharing Experience" (see Figure 7.2, Chapter 7) to understand how teachers communicate to develop consensus with regard to how they should teach the pupils. Mercer's (2004) theory of the use of language could be also be presented in connection with this category. Mercer describes three levels when it comes to the use of language in conversation, and these levels indicate whether the sharing of experience will promote learning or not. Mercer's theoretical standpoint is socio-cultural theory, and this theory could therefore fit very well if the researcher has the same theory reference framework, which may comprise all social-constructivist theories. This "theoretical analysis" (Postholm, 2010) starts with the data material and does not stray from it. The interpretation, however, does. In the interpretation the researcher can indicate implications of the study based on the analysis that has been made. For example, what does the sharing of experience mean for the teacher, how should this sharing be organised and how should the language be used to promote learning? These are questions the researcher can discuss in a final interpretation section in the chapter based on this category. I thus place interpretation and discussion on equal footing based on the preceding analysis. A chapter based on a category can therefore be structured as presented in Figure 9.1.

| Theory | Empirical findings | Analysis | Interpretation/Discussion |

FIGURE 9.1   Structure of a chapter

When theory and related research are presented in a separate chapter and even more theory and research presented in the findings chapters, the researcher should give grounds for choosing to structure the text in this way. One rationale may be that it will be simpler to follow the analysis if some of the theory and related research have been presented in close connection with the empirical findings in the analysis chapter.

7 Descriptions as the Starting Point for Further Analysis

If the researcher has collected comprehensive data material during the research or DWR project, he or she can first write a thorough description which is presented as part of the findings section. This description can then serve as the foundation for developing categories the researcher wants to zoom in on and analyse and interpret, as shown in the figure above. In the research carried out in the UiU programme when it was nearing its end, I (Postholm, 2018c) conducted research in three schools, and in the findings section I presented thorough descriptions of the activity in each school, as well as thoughts and reflections on these activities. Observations of a teacher, below called the "shadowed teacher", and interviews with teachers, pupils and leaders contributed data material to these descriptions. Below I reproduce what I (Postholm, 2018c) wrote to invite the reader into the classroom to show how varied and practical teaching was carried out.

> The pupils in the 9B class, 11 boys and 13 girls, are going to review the short story "Karen" by Norwegian author Alexander Kjelland. The teacher asks which group this author belongs to, and a pupil responds "the big four" [term often used about the Norwegian authors Ibsen, Bjørnson, Kjelland and Garborg]. The teacher draws a tavern, Krarup tavern, on the board, and asks if one of the pupils would like to draw Karen, the servant girl. One of the boys raises his hand, and is allowed to go to the board to draw her. The boy draws Karen in a narrow blue dress (she was pregnant) and with a large bosom, causing the pupils to laugh. Another pupil draws the tavern owner, and yet another pupil draws the post-wagon driver and postman arriving with horse and carriage. The teacher talks while the pupils draw and also asks the pupils questions, so the content and message of the text are repeated, as is the point or message of the short story. In the next class they will talk about the importance of this short story in today's society. (p. 104)

Next in the description based on this study I (Postholm, 2018c) examine "the shadowed teacher and the teachers' experiences and learning", "the pupils' experiences and learning" and "the experiences and learning of the school leaders". In the analysis across the three schools I zoom in on "contextual factors and learning" as the main category and with the sub categories "start-up and anchoring", "sharing culture and cooperation with colleagues" and "the leader's role". The next main category was "learning on all levels" with the sub-categories "teachers' learning", "pupils' learning" "leaders' learning" and "lasting traces". A final chapter is based on the main research question and the sub-questions for the study. This chapter also points out implications for future school development activities based on findings from the study. This is a joint chapter (Postholm et al., 2018), as the study of the UiU programme was conducted as several sub-studies answering the same research questions. In a Master's thesis this final chapter will be a summary of findings answering the research questions that were asked in the introduction. This thesis will also suggest future research, as Merriam (2002) proposes, which is a sign of a well-written study.

In the analyses of the comprehensive material from three schools I (Postholm, 2018b) have first used a phenomenological analysis (Giorgi, 1985; Moustakas, 1994) to produce a description of each school. These descriptions then form the basis for an analysis across the schools using the constant comparative analysis method (Strauss & Corbin, 1990, 1998). In a Master's thesis the data material will probably not be so comprehensive so that categories can be developed directly according to the transcriptions through, for example, constant comparative analysis. When using only one analytical method, the researcher will only have to describe this one method in the methods section, which is sufficient and also best for a Master's degree student learning analysis of data material.

8 Quotations Embedded in the Text

In Chapter 3 I wrote that qualitative research elicits the research participants' perspective (Creswell, 2013; Denzin & Lincoln, 2011). This can be achieved if the researcher paraphrases their opinions or includes their voices by embedding quotations in the text. Quotations may be presented in different ways. Below I present quotations from school research that I (Postholm, 2018c) carried out in response to the main research question and the sub-questions presented above. A quotation that is less than three lines can be embedded in the main body of the text and then highlighted with quotation marks as follows: "We have seen that school-based development work is the correct path to take, if school is to raise its competence, the whole school must join in raising competence over time", the principal states (p. 113). A quotation longer than three lines can be written as a separate paragraph with left indentation as seen below. A teacher has the following to say:

> You can't have a rock concert every time you have a class. Because I believe that the pupils, even if they will readily admit that close reading of a paragraph in the book is useful, will nevertheless find it boring. But if we can do this in between doing other things I think the sum of this will be learning. (p. 105)

The voices of the research participants can also be reproduced in dialogues. Below is a dialogue between the teacher Gunhild and the researcher:

Gunhild: I'm thinking about the conversation we had with you (the researcher) yesterday (the focus-group interview with two teachers teaching Years 8, 9 and 10). What if we could have somebody come in more frequently and get us to talk like that?

Researcher: That was interesting to hear.

Gunhild: You wouldn't get the same effect if I were to guide a colleague. I think it's more important to have somebody from the outside asking questions that make us think and discuss. Then we will have more of a meta-perspective on what we're doing. It would have been more efficient than all these time limits and all these assignments.

Researcher: You find it important that somebody from the outside comes to your school?

Gunhild I've been saying this over and over again, just the fact that you're here now. I've joined in all the conversations you have had with the others. I have had much better conversations and reflections with my colleagues than for years. Getting somebody to come in, asking questions, it makes us think. Why don't we think of using this more. Because this is important.
And if we do it in-house, then it becomes like nit-picking. Going in circles, you know. Because it's perceived as criticism if you say something. (p. 140)

As seen above, the voices of the research participants can be presented in embedded quotations in the text body, can be separated as a longer statement and can be presented as a dialogue. The researcher can also paraphrase what the participants have said.

9 The Connecting Theme in the Master's Thesis

Based on what I have said about structure of a Master's thesis I present a summary of the structure in Figure 9.2.

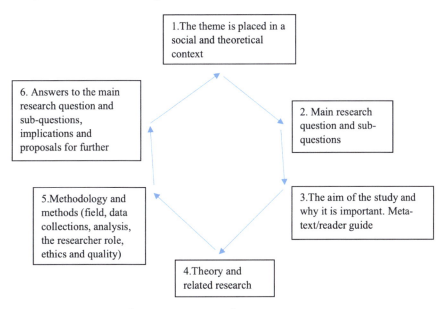

FIGURE 9.2 Structure and content in a Master's thesis

When presenting a study, it should be shown that there is a close connection between the researcher's theoretical stance and the main research question and sub-questions asked. When the researcher places the theme of the study in a social context in the introduction, the relevance and therefore the aim of the study and why it is important will also be explained. The overarching theory and relevant earlier research are presented separately or in the same chapter for further placement of the study in a theoretical tradition and to present some of the existing knowledge on the theme before conducting the study. A Master's degree student is not expected to present a complete overview of earlier studies in the field, but the student should have some knowledge about research connected to the theme that is the focus of the study. The methodology chosen and how the researcher will proceed should also be consistent with the main research question and sub-questions so that the findings in the study will answer the questions asked. When the researcher manages to connect the different phases and content elements together a connecting theme can be established in the research process and in the written presentation of it. It is important for the researcher to give reasons for all the choices made in the research process so that the connecting theme appears clearly in connection with the choices made. When writing a Master's thesis, students are also required to comply with formal guidelines.

Note

1 In Chapter 7 I presented categories which were developed according to a pilot study that ran through the autumn of 2012 and the spring of 2013.

APPENDIX 1

Sample Letter of Consent

May Britt Postholm
for the Coordination Group for *Nettverk for Kompetansemiljøer* [Network for Competence Communities]
c/o Department of Education
Norwegian University of Science and Technology
N-7491 Trondheim   Date

To
School leaders
Teachers

1   Research on *Ungdomstrinn i utvikling* [Lower Secondary Stage in Development]

1.1   *Background*

Ungdomstrinn i utvikling (UiU – lower secondary stage in development) is a national programme focusing specifically on lower secondary school. The purpose of the programme is that pupils will experience teaching that is relevant, practical, varied and challenging so that they experience mastery and will be motivated for school work. In the 2012/2013 school year a pilot programme for this effort was carried out in selected schools and teacher education institutions in Norway.

    The Coordination Group for the Competence Communities at the Norwegian University of Science and Technology researched this pilot programme and findings from this research have been published in a book (Postholm et al., 2013). The aim of the pilot project and the research on it has been to advise and give direction to the full-scale project which was launched in the autumn of 2013 with completion at the end of 2017. The official project period is thus nearing its completion. The Norwegian Directorate for Education and Training has asked the Coordination Group to write a full report on the impact of the programme.

1.2   *Research, Data Collection and Publication*

The Coordination Group wants to conduct new research in order to study the experiences of school leaders, teachers, pupils, school owners and teacher educators with this programme and the impact it has had on learning and development in school and in the teaching. We would like to study what the participants have learnt, how they learnt and how the learning is expressed in the participants' practices. The overarching main thesis question in the study is: *What importance has UiU had for development on different levels in school and education?* To answer this question we will use a qualitative study to collect data as follows:

- Observation or shadowing of a teacher (main informant) for up to one week (Year 9)
- Semi-structured interview with the main informant
- Observation of and focus-group interview with the main informant's team
- Focus-group interview with pupils (who the main informant is responsible for)
- Focus-group interview with school leaders
- Focus-group interview with two teachers from each of the three stages in the school
- Letter written by all the teachers
- Focus-group interview with teacher educators

Data collection and data processing will comply with the requirements established in the Personal Information Act and with research ethics principles. Informed consent will be obtained from all the research participants, and all material collected will be made anonymous. The research findings will be published in a report to the Norwegian Directorate for Education and Training and in scientific articles and book chapters.

We hope you will be willing to participate!

Yours sincerely
May Britt Postholm
On behalf of the Coordination Group

Response slip:

I would like to participate in this research project and give my consent to using the collected material for research purposes.

_____

Name and institution/affiliation

APPENDIX 2

Interview Guide for Shadowed Teachers

- What is your education background?
- How long have you worked as a teacher?
- Which subjects do you teach?
- Which years in primary school have you taught?
- How do you experience your own role when it comes to your colleagues' learning and development of teaching?
- How did the school arrive at the topic for development work?
- Was a plan made for the work in this programme? If so, can you describe its content?
- How did the teachers and leaders become aware of the current situation in the teaching in relation to the chosen focus of the development work?
- How did the school develop an overarching goal for the programme?
- How did this overarching goal gain importance for the activity in the classroom?
- Were sub-goals (development goals) developed to be worked with in the teaching? If yes, please elaborate.
- How do you understand practical, varied, relevant and challenging teaching?
- How do you plan your teaching to motivate all or as many of your pupils as possible to learn?
- How important is it to you to cooperate with colleagues on your own learning and teaching?
- How important do you feel the school leaders are for the teachers' learning and teaching? (timetable – organisation and content of meetings)
- How do you experience you own role when it comes to your colleagues' learning and development of teaching?
- How do you experience that UiU has contributed to the collective learning in school? (for better learning for the pupils)
- Do you find that school-based competence development has had impact on the culture in your school? If so, how? (values, norms, perceptions, attitudes, relationships, the learning environment of teachers and pupils)

APPENDIX 3

Overview of Data Material Collected in School A1

1   **Interview**

27 February 2017: Interview with the leader team:
Focus-group interview with the leader team. Focus: experiences of participation in UiU. Here something should be stated about the content of the interview – which questions were asked.

28 February 2017: Focus-group interview with the team the teacher shadowed for a week belongs to. Here something should be stated about the content of the interview.

1 March 2017: Focus-group interview with two teachers from each Year in lower secondary school. Here something should be stated about the content of the interview.

3 March 2017: Focus-group interview with the shadowed teacher. Here something should be stated about the content of the interview.

2   **Observation**

2 March 2017: Observation of Norwegian language department meeting. Here something should be stated about the content of the observations.

28 February 2017: Observation of class in music (Year 9, group 1). Here something should be stated about the content of the observations.

28 February 2017: Observation of class in music (Year 9, group 2). Here something should be stated about the content of the observations.

1 March 2017: Observation of class in music (Year 9, group 1). Here something should be stated about the content of the observations.

1 March 2017: Observation of class in music (Year 9, group 2). Here something should be stated about the content of the observations.

1 March 2017: Observation of KRLE (Christian and other religious and ethical education) (Year 9). Here something should be stated about the content of the observations.

APPENDICES

1 March 2017:	Observation class in Norwegian (Year 9). Here something should be stated about the content of the observations.
2 March 2017:	Mental health, double class (Year 10). Here something should be stated about the content of the observations.
3 March 2017:	Mental health, double class (Year 10). Here something should be stated about the content of the observations.
Letter method:	Letter sent to school in advance before the research started. The principal had collected answers to the questions in the letters the teachers had answered in writing.

References

Adler, P. A., & Adler, P. (1994). Observational techniques. In N. K. Denzin & Y. S. Lincoln (Eds.), *Handbook of qualitative research* (pp. 377–392). Thousand Oaks, CA: Sage Publications, Inc.

Altheide, D. L., & Johnson, J. M. (2011). Reflections on the interpretive adequacy in qualitative research. In N. K. Denzin & Y. S. Lincoln (Eds.), *The Sage handbook of qualitative research* (pp. 581–594). Los Angeles, CA: Sage Publications, Inc.

Alvesson, M., & Sköldberg, K. (2009). *Reflexive methodology: 2 new vistas for qualitative research* (2nd ed.). London: Sage Publications, Inc.

Angrosino, M. V., & de Peréz, K. A. M. (2000). Rethinking observation: From method to context. In N. K Denzin & Y. S. Lincoln (Eds.), *Handbook of qualitative research* (2nd ed., pp. 467–478). Thousand Oaks, CA: Sage Publications, Inc.

Angrosino, M. V., & Rosenberg, J. (2000). Observations on observation. Continuities and challenges. In N. K Denzin & Y. S. Lincoln (Eds.), *Handbook of qualitative research* (2nd ed., pp. 673–702). Thousand Oaks, CA: Sage Publications, Inc.

Avalos, B. (2011). Teacher professional development in teaching and teacher education over ten years. *Teaching and Teacher Education, 27*(1), 10–20.

Bakhtin, M. (1981). *The dialogic imagination* (M. Holquist, Ed.). Austin, TX: University of Texas Press.

Bakhtin, M. (1986). *Speech genres & other late essays* (C. Emerson & M. Holquist, Eds.). Austin, TX: University of Texas Press.

Bateson, G. (1972). *Steps to an ecology of mind: A revolutionary approach to man's understanding of himself.* New York, NY: Ballantine.

Bjørndal, C. R. P. (2011). Rådgiver eller veileder [Counsellor or Supervisor]. In K. Skagen (Ed.), *Kunnskap og handling i pedagogisk veiledning* [Knowledge and action in pedagogical supervision] (2nd ed., pp. 189–212). Bergen: Fagbokforlaget.

Boekaerts, M., Pintrich, P., & Zeidner, M. (2000). Self-regulation: An introductory review. In M. Boekarts, P. R. Pintrich, & M. Zeidner (Eds.), *Handbook of self-regulation* (pp. 1–9). San Diego, CA: Academic Press.

Bogden, R. C., & Biklen, S. K. (2007). *Qualitative research for education. An introduction to theory and methods.* Boston, MA: Pearson.

Burke, K. (1935). *Permanence and change.* New York, NY: New Republic.

Charmaz, K. (2014). *Constructing grounded theory* (2nd ed.). London: Sage Publications, Inc.

Chrzanowska, J. (2002). *Interviewing groups and individuals in qualitative market research.* Thousand Oaks, CA: Sage Publications, Inc.

Clandinin, D. J., & Connelly, F. M. (2000). *Narrative inquiry: Experience and story in qualitative research.* San Francisco, CA: Jossey-Bass.

City, E. A., Elmore, R. F., Fiarman, R. F., & Tietel, L. (2010). *instructional rounds in education: A network approach to improving teaching and learning*. Cambridge, MA: Harvard Education Press.

Coghlan, D., & Brannick, T. (2005). *Doing action research in your own organization*. London: Sage Publications, Inc.

Cole, M. (1996). *Cultural psychology: A once and future discipline*. Cambridge, MA: The Belknap Press of Harvard University Press.

Cole, M., & Engeström, Y. (2007). Cultural-historical approaches to designing for development. In J. Valsiner & A. Rosa (Eds.), *The Cambridge handbook of sociocultural psychology* (pp. 484–507). New York, NY: Cambridge University Press.

Corbin, J., & Strauss, A. (2008). *Basics of qualitative research*. Los Angeles, CA: Sage Publications, Inc.

Creswell, J. W. (2013). *Qualitative inquiry & research design: Choosing among five approaches* (3rd ed.). Los Angeles, CA: Sage Publications, Inc.

Czarniawaska, B. (2004). *Narratives in social science research*. Thousand Oaks, CA: Sage Publications.

Denzin, N. K. (1989). *Interpretive biography*. Newbury Park, CA: Sage Publications.

Denzin, N. K., & Lincoln, Y. S. (2011). Introduction: The discipline and practice of qualitative research. In N. K. Denzin & Y. S. Lincoln (Eds.), *The Sage handbook of qualitative research* (4th ed., pp. 1–19). Los Angeles, CA: Sage Publications, Inc.

Dewey, J. (1916). *Democracy and education. An introduction to the philosophy of education*. New York, NY: Macmillan Company.

Dewey, J. (1920). *Reconstruction in philosophy*. New York, NY: Henry Holt and Company.

Directorate of Education and Training. (2012). *Rammeverk for skolebasert kompetanseutvikling på ungdomstrinnet 2012–2017* [General framework for school-based competence raising at the lower secondary school level 2012–2017]. Oslo: Utdanningsdirektoratet.

Dukes, S. (1984). Phenomenological methodology in the human sciences. *Journal of Religion and Health, 23*(3), 197–203. doi:10.1007/BF00990785

Eisner, E. (1997). The promise and perils of alternative forms of data representation. *Educational Researcher, 26*(6), 4–10. doi:10.3102/0013189X026006004

Engeström, Y. (1987). *Learning by expanding*. Helsinki: Orienta-Konsultit Oy.

Engeström, Y. (1999). Activity theory and individual and social transformation. In Y. Engeström, R. Miettinen, & R. Punamaki (Eds.), *Perspectives on activity theory* (pp. 19–38). Cambridge, MA: Cambridge University Press.

Engeström, Y. (2000). From individual action to collective activity and back: Developmental work research as an interventionist methodology. In P. Lauff, J. Hindmarsh, & C. Heath (Eds.), *Workplace studies. Recovering work and informing system design* (pp. 150–280). New York, NY: Cambridge University Press.

Engeström, Y. (2001). *Expansive learning at work. Toward an activity-theoretical reconceptualization.* London: Institute of Education, University of London.

Engeström, Y. (2007). Putting Vygotsky to work. The change laboratory as an application of double stimulation. In H. Daniels, M. Cole, & J. V. Wertsch (Eds.). *The Cambridge companion to Vygotsky* (pp. 363–382). Cambridge, MA: Cambridge University Press.

Engeström, Y., & Engeström, R. (1986). Developmental work research. The approach and the application in cleaning work. *Nordisk Pedagogik, 6,* 2–15.

Engeström, Y., & Miettinen, R. (1999). Introduction. In Y. Engeström, R. Miettinen, & R. Punamaki (Eds.), *Perspectives on activity theory* (pp. 1–16). Cambridge, MA: Cambridge University Press.

Engeström, Y., & Sannino, A. (2010). Studies of expansive learning: Foundations, findings and future challenges. *Educational Research Review, 5*(1), 1–24. doi:10.1016/j.edurev.2009.12.002

Erickson, F. (1986). Qualitative methods in research on teaching. In M. C. Wittrock (Ed.), *Handbook of research on teaching* (pp. 119–161). New York, NY: MacMillan Publishing Company.

Erickson, F. (2011). The history of qualitative inquiry in social and educational research. In N. K. Denzin & Y. S. Lincoln (Eds.), *The Sage handbook of qualitative research* (pp. 43–59). Los Angeles, CA: Sage Publications, Inc.

Fetterman, D. M. (2010). *Ethnography: Step by step* (3rd ed.). Thousand Oaks, CA: Sage Publications.

Flavell, J. H. (1979). Metacognition and cognitive monitoring: A new area of cognitive developmental inquiry. *American Psychologist, 34,* 906–911.

Flavell, J. H. (1987). Speculations about the nature and development of metacognition. In F. E. Weinert & R. H. Kluwe (Eds.), *Metacognition, motivation, and understanding* (pp. 21–29). Hillsdale, NJ: Erlbaum.

Fontana, A., & Frey, J. H. (2000). From structured questions to negotiated text. In N. K. Denzin & Y. S. Lincoln (Eds.), *Handbook of qualitative research* (2nd ed., pp. 645–672). Thousand Oaks, CA: Sage Publications, Inc.

Gadamer, H.-G. (2012). *Sannhet og metode: grunntrekk i en filosofisk hermeneutikk* [Truth and method: basic features of a philosophical hermeneutics]. Oslo: Pax.

Geertz, C. (1973). *The interpretation of cultures: Selected essays.* New York, NY: Basic Books.

Gergen, K. J. (1995). Social construction and the education process. In L. D. Steffe & J. Gale (Eds.), *Constructivism in education* (pp. 17–40). Hillsdale, NJ: Lawrence Erlbaum.

Gibbs, G. (2015). *Analyzing qualitative data.* Los Angeles, CA: Sage Publications.

Gilgun, J. F. (2005). "Grab" and good science: Writing up the results of qualitative research. *Qualitative Health Research, 15,* 256–262. doi:10.1177/1049732304268796

Giorgi, A. (1985). *Phenomenology and psychological research.* Pittsburgh, PA: Duquesne University Press.

Glaser, B., & Strauss, A. (1967). *The discovery of grounded theory.* Chicago, IL: Aldine.

Glesne, C. (2011). *Becoming qualitative researchers: An introduction* (3rd ed.). Boston, MA: Pearson/Allyn & Bacon.

Gold, R. L. (1958). Roles in sociological field observation. *Social Forces, 36,* 217–223.

Greenwood, D. J., & Levin, M. (2007). *Introduction to action research. Social research for social change* (2nd ed.). Thousand Oaks, CA: Sage Publications, Inc.

Guba, E. (1981). Criteria for assessing the trustworthiness of naturalistic inquiries. *Educational Communication and Technology Journal, 29,* 75–92. doi:10.1007/BF02766777

Guba, E., & Lincoln, Y. S. (1988). Do inquiry paradigms imply inquiry methodologies? In D. M. Fetterman (Ed.), *Qualitative approaches to evaluation in education* (pp. 89–115). New York, NY: Praeger.

Guba, E. G., & Lincoln, Y. S. (1989). *Fourth generation evaluation.* Newbury Park, CA: Sage Publications, Inc.

Gudmundsdottir, S. (1992). Den kvalitative forskningsprosessen [The qualitative research process]. *Norsk pedagogisk tidsskrift, 5,* 266–276.

Gudmundsdottir, S. (1997). Narrativ forskning på pedagogisk praksis [Narrative research of pedagogical practice]. In B. Karseth, S. Gudmundsdottir, & S. Hopmann (Eds.), *Didaktikk: Tradisjon og fornyelse. Festskrift til Bjørg Brandtzæg Gundem* [Didactics: Tradition and renewal. Memorial publication for Bjørg Brandtzæg Gundem] (pp. 147–172). Oslo: University of Oslo, PFI.

Gudmundsdottir, S. (2001). Narrative research in school practice. In V. Richardson (Ed.), *Fourth handbook for research on teaching* (pp. 226–240). New York, NY: Macmillan.

Hammersley, M., & Atkinson, P. (2007). *Ethnography: Principles in practice* (3rd ed.). New York, NY: Routledge.

Heshusius, L. (1994). Freeing ourselves from objectivity: Managing subjectivity or turning toward a participatory mode of consciousness? *Educational Researcher, 23*(3), 15–22. doi:10.3102/0013189X023003015

Husserl, E. (1983). *Ideas pertaining to a pure phenomenology and to a phenomenological philosophy* (Book 1., F. Kersten, Trans.). The Hague: Martinus Nijhoff. (Orig. pub. German, 1913)

Junge, J. (2012). Læreres bruk av narrative i kollegasamtaler [Teachers' use of narrative in mentor talk]. *Nordic Studies in Education, 2,* 126–138.

Kamberelis, G., & Dimitriadis, G. (2011). Focus Groups. Contingent articulations of pedagogy, politics, and inquiry. In N. K. Denzin & Y. S. Lincoln (Eds.), *Handbook of qualitative research* (4th ed., pp. 545–561). Thousand Oaks, CA: Sage Publications, Inc.

Kerlinger, F. N. (1979). *Behavioral research.* New York, NY: Holt, Rhinehhart, & Winston.

Kluckhohn, C. (1949). *Mirror for man. The relation of anthropology to modern life.* New York, NY: Whittlesey House, Inc.

Kuhn, T. (1970). *The Structure of scientific revolutions*. Chicago, IL: The University of Chicago Press.

Kvale, S., & Brinkmann, S. (2015). *Det kvalitative forskningsintervju* [The qualitative research interview] (3rd ed.). Oslo: Gyldendal Norsk Forlag.

Lektorsky, V. A. (1980). *Subject object cognition*. Moscow: Progress Publishers.

Leont'ev, A. N. (1978). *Activity, consciousness, and personality*. Englewood Cliffs, NJ: Prentice-Hall.

Leont'ev, A. N. (1981). The problem of activity in psychology. In J. V. Wertsch (Ed.), *The concept of activity in soviet psychology* (pp. 37–71). Armonk: M.E. Sharpe, Inc.

Lincoln, Y. S., & Guba, E. G. (1985). *Naturalistic inquiry*. Beverly Hills, CA: Sage Publications, Inc.

Lincoln, Y. S., & Guba, E. G. (2000). The only generalization is: There is no generalization. In R. Gomm, M. Hammersley, & P. Foster (Eds.), *Case study method. Key issues, key text* (pp. 27–40). Thousand Oaks, CA: Sage Publications, Inc.

Lincoln, Y. S., Lynham, S. A., & Guba, E. G. (2011). Paradigmatic controversies, contradictions, and emerging confluences, revisited. In N. K. Denzin & Y. S. Lincoln (Eds.), *The Sage handbook of qualitative research* (pp. 97–128). Los Angeles, CA: Sage Publications, Inc.

Luria, A. R. (1928). The problem of the cultural development of the child. *Journal of Genetic Psychology, 35*, 493–506.

Lynton, N. (1980). *The story of modern art*. Oxford: Phaidon.

Malinowski, B. (1922). *Argonauts of the Western Pacific*. London: Routledge.

Mayer, R. E. (1996). Learners as information processors: Legacies and limitations of educational psychology's second metaphor. *Educational Psychologist, 31*(3–4), 151–161. doi:10.1080/00461520.1996.9653263

Mead, M. (1928). *Coming of age in Samoa: A psychological study of primitive youth of Western civilization*. New York, NY: William Morrow.

Mercer, N. (2004). Sociocultural discourse analysis: Analysing classroom talk as a social mode of thinking. *Journal of Applied Linguistics, 1*(2), 137–168.

Merriam, S. B. (1998). *Qualitative research and case study applications in education*. San Francisco, CA: Jossey-Bass.

Merriam, S. B. (2009). *Qualitative research: A guide to design and implementation*. San Francisco, CA: Jossey-Bass.

Merriam, S. B., & Associates. (2002). Introduction to qualitative research. In S. B. Merriam (Ed.), *Qualitative research in practice* (pp. 3–17). San Francisco, CA: Jossey-Bass.

Merton, R. (1967). *On theoretical sociology*. New York, NY: Free Press.

Middleton, D. (2010). Identifying learning in interprofessional discourse. The development of an analytic protocol. In H. Daniels, A. Edwards, Y. Engeström, T. Gallagher, & S. Ludvigsen (Eds.), *Activity theory in practice. Promoting learning and across boundaries and agencies* (pp. 90–104). London: Routledge.

REFERENCES

Ministry of Education and Research. (2011). *Meld. St. 22 (2010–2011) Motivasjon – Mestring – Muligheter* [White paper No. 22: Motivation – Mastering – Possibilities]. Oslo: Kunnskapsdepartementet.

Ministry of Education and Research. (2012). *Strategi for ungdomstrinnet- Motivasjon og mestring for bedre læring. Felles satsing på klasseledelse, regning, lesing og skriving* [Strategies for the lower secondary school stage: Motivation and mastering for better learning. Joint effort on classroom management, reading, writing and arithmetic]. Oslo: Kunnskapsdepartementet.

Moustakas, C. (1994). *Phenomenological research methods*. Thousand Oaks, CA: Sage Publications, Inc.

Muncey, T. (2010). *Creating autoethnographies*. Los Angeles, CA: Sage Publications, Inc.

Ormiston, G., & Schrift, A. (1990). Introduction. In G. Ormiston & A. Schrift (Eds.), *The hermeneutic tradition* (pp. 1–35). New York, NY: SUNY Press.

Patton, M. Q. (2002). *Qualitative research & evaluation methods* (3rd ed.). Thousand Oaks, CA: Sage Publications, Inc.

Pintrich, P. R. (2000). The role of goal orientation in self-regulated learning. In M. Boekarts, P. R. Pintrich, & M. Zeidner (Eds.), *Handbook of self-regulation* (pp. 451–502). San Diego, CA: Academic Press.

Polkinghorne, D. E. (1989). Phenomenological research methods. In R. S. Valle & S. Halling (Eds.), *Existential-phenomenological perspectives in psychology* (pp. 41–60). New York, NY: Plenum.

Postholm, M. B. (2008a). The start-up phase in a research and development work project: A foundation for development. *Teaching and Teacher Education, 24*(3), 575–584. doi:10.1016/j.tate.2007.08.001

Postholm, M. B. (2008b). Teachers developing practice: Reflection as key activity. *Teaching and Teacher Education, 24*(7), 1717–1728. doi:10.1016/j.tate.2008.02.024

Postholm, M. B. (2010). *Kvalitativ metode. En innføring med fokus på fenomenologi, etnografi og kasusstudier* [Qualitative method. An introduction focusing on phenomenology, ethnography and case studies] (2nd ed.). Oslo: Universitetsforlaget.

Postholm, M. B. (2012). Teachers' professional development: A theoretical review: *Educational Research, 54*(4), 405–429. doi:10.1080/00131881.2012.734725

Postholm, M. B. (2013). Den nærværende og forskende lærer [The present and researching teacher]. In M. Brekke & T. Tiller (Ed.), *Læreren som forsker. Innføring i forskningsarbeid i skolen* [The teacher as researcher. Introduction to research work in school] (pp. 62–78). Oslo: Universitetsforlaget.

Postholm, M. P. (2018a). Teachers' professional development in school: A review study. *Cogent Education*. https://doi.org/10.1080/2331186X.2018.1522781

Postholm, M. B. (2018b). Vedlegg 1 [Appendix 1]. In M. B. Postholm, A. Normann, T. Dahl, E. Dehlin, G. Engvik, & E. J. Irgens (Eds.), *Skole- og utdanningssektoren i utvikling* [The school and education sector in development] (pp. 323–335). Bergen: Fagbokforlaget.

Postholm, M. B. (2018c). Case A [Case A]. In M. B. Postholm, A. Normann, T. Dahl, E. Dehlin, G. Engvik, & E. J. Irgens (Eds.), *Skole- og utdanningssektoren i utvikling* [The school and education sector in development] (pp. 99–162). Bergen: Fagbokforlaget.

Postholm, M. B. Dahl, T., Dehlin, E., Engvik, G., Irgens, E. J., & Normann, A. (2018). Forskningens design [Research Design]. In M. B. Postholm, A. Normann, T. Dahl, E. Dehlin, G. Engvik, & E. J. Irgens (Eds.), *Skole- og utdanningssektoren i utvikling* [The school and education sector in development] (pp. 93–98). Bergen: Fagbokforlaget.

Postholm, M. B., Dahl, T., Engvik, G., Fjørtoft, H., Irgens, E. J., Sandvik, L., & Wæge, K. (2013). *En gavepakke til ungdomstrinnet? En undersøkelse av piloten for den nasjonale satsingen på skolebasert kompetanseutvikling* [Gift-wrapped for lower-secondary school? A study of the pilot project for the national effort for school-based competence development]. Trondheim: Akademika.

Postholm, M. B., & Jacobsen, D. I. (2011). *Læreren med forskerblikk. En innføringsbok i vitenskapelig metode for lærerstudenter* [The teacher with the researcher's gaze. An introductory book in scientific methods for teaching students]. Kristiansand: Høyskoleforlaget.

Postholm, M. B., & Madsen, J. (2006). The researcher's role: An ethical dimension. *Outlines, 7*(1), 49–60.

Postholm, M. B., & Moen, T. (2011). Communities of development: A new model for R&D work. *Journal of Educational Change, 12*(4) 385–401. Retrieved from https://link.springer.com/article/10.1007/s10833-010-9150-x

Postholm, M. B. Normann, A., Dahl, T., Dehlin, E., Engvik, G., & Irgens, E. J. (2018). Lærerutdanning, nasjonale sentra og ungdomstrinn i utvikling. Læring og implikasjoner for rammer og organisering av framtidig utviklingsarbeid [Teacher training, national centres and lower secondary school in development. Teaching and implications for frameworks and organization of future development work]. In M. B. Postholm, A. Normann, T. Dahl, E. Dehlin, G. Engvik, & E. J. Irgens (Eds.), *Skole- og utdanningssektoren i utvikling* [The school and education sector in development] (pp. 299–319). Bergen: Fagbokforlaget.

Postholm, M. B., & Skrøvset, S. (2013). The researcher reflecting on her own role during action research. *Educational Action Research Journal, 21*(4), 506–518. doi:10.1080/09650792.2013.833798

Postholm, M. B., Wold Granum, M., & Gudmundsdottir, S. (1999). *"Det her er vanskelig, altså". En kasusstudie av prosjektarbeid* [This is quite difficult. A case study of project work]. Trondheim: Tapir Akademisk Forlag.

Postholm, M. B., & Wæge, K. (2016). Teachers' learning in school-based development. *Educational Research, 58*(1), 24–38. doi:10.1080/00131881.2015.1117350

REFERENCES

Prawat, R. S. (1996). Constructivisms, modern and postmodern. *Educational Psychologist, 31*(3–4), 191–206. doi:10.1080/00461520.1996.9653268

Revans, R. W. (1982). *The origins and growth of action learning.* Bromley: Chartwell-Bratt Ltd.

Revans, R. W. (1984). *The sequence of managerial achievement.* Bradford: MCB University Press.

Riessman, C. K. (2008). *Narrative methods for the human sciences.* Los Angeles, CA: Sage Publications, Inc.

Richardson, L. (1994). Writing: A method of inquiry. In N. K. Denzin & Y. S. Lincoln (Eds.), *Handbook of qualitative research* (pp. 516–529). Thousand Oaks, CA: Sage Publications.

Richardson, L., & St. Pierre, E. A. (2005). Writing: A method of inquiry. In N. K. Denzin & Y. S. Lincoln (Eds.), *The Sage handbook of qualitative research* (3rd ed., pp. 959–978). Thousand Oaks, CA: Sage Publications, Inc.

Ricoeur, P. (1981). *Hermeneutics and the human sciences.* Cambridge: Cambridge University Press.

Rorty, R. (1989). *Contingency, irony, and solidarity.* Cambridge: Cambridge University Press.

Rubin, H. J., & Rubin, I. S. (2005). *Qualitative Interviewing. The art of hearing data* (2nd ed.). Thousand Oaks, CA: Sage Publications.

Ry Nielsen, J. C., & Repstad, P. (2006). Når mauren også skal være ørn [When the ant shall also be the eagle]. In F. Nyeng & G. Wennes (Eds.), *Tall, tolkning og tvil bak metodevalg i økonomi, ledelse og markedsføring* [Numbers, interpretation and doubt behind the choice of method in economics, management and marketing] (pp. 245–279). Oslo: Cappelen Akademisk forlag.

Sacks, H. (1992). *Lectures on conversation* (Vol. I and II). Oxford: Blackwell.

Sacks, H., Schegloff, E., & Jefferson, G. (1974). A simplest systematics for the organization of turn-taking in conversation. *Language, 50*, 696–735.

Savin-Baden, M., & Major, C. H. (2013). *Qualitative research. The essential guide to theory and practice.* London: Routledge.

Säljö, R. (1999). Learning as the use of tools. A sociocultural perspective on the human-technology link. In K. Littleton & P. Light (Eds.), *Learning with computers. Analysing productive interaction* (pp. 144–161). New York, NY: Routledge.

Shulman, L. S. (1981). Disciplines of inquiry in education: An overview. *Educational Researcher, 10*(6), 5–12.

Spindler, G. (1955). *Education and anthropology.* Stanford, CA: Stanford University Press.

Stake, R. E. (1995). *The art of case studies.* Thousand Oaks, CA: Sage Publications, Inc.

Stake, R. E., & Trumbull, D. (1982). Naturalistic generalization. *Review Journal of Philosophy and Social Science, 7*(1), 1–12.

Strauss, A., & Corbin, J. (1990). *Basics of qualitative research: Grounded theory procedures and techniques.* Newbury Park, CA: Sage Publications, Inc.

Strauss, A., & Corbin, J. (1998). *Basics of qualitative research: Techniques and procedures for developing grounded theory.* Thousand Oaks, CA: Sage Publications, Inc.

Tholander, M., & Cekaite, A. (2015). Konversasjonsanalys [Conversation Analysis]. In A. Fejes & R. Thornberg (Eds.), *Handbok i kvalitativ analys* [Handbook of qualitative analysis] (pp. 194–1217). Stockholm: Liber AB.

Tierney, W. G. (1997). Lost in translation: Time and voice in qualitative research. In W. G. Tierney & Y. S. Lincoln (Eds.), *Representation and the text: Re-framing the narrative voice* (pp. 23–36). Albany, NY: SUNY Press.

Timperley, H., Wilson, A., Barrar, H., & Fung, I. (2007). *Teacher professional learning and development: Best evidence synthesis iteration.* Wellington: Ministry of Education.

Van Manen, M. (1990). *Researching lived experiences. Human science for an action sensitive pedagogy* (2nd ed.). Waterloo: The Althouse Press.

Van Manen, M. (2016). *Phenomenology of practice. Meaning-giving methods in phenomenological research and writing.* London: Routledge.

Volosinov, V. N. (1973). *Marxism and the philosophy of language.* New York, NY: Seminar Press.

Vygotsky, L. S. (1978). *Mind in society. The development of higher psychological processes.* Cambridge, MA: Harvard University Press.

Vygotsky, L. S. (1997). Research method (chapter 2). In *The collected works of L.S. Vygotsky, vol 4. The history of the development of higher mental functions* (pp. 27–63). New York, NY: Plenum Press.

Vygotsky, L. S. (2000). *Thought and language.* Cambridge, MA: MIT Press.

Wardekker, W. (2000). Criteria for the quality of inquiry. *Mind, Culture, and Activity,* 7(4), 259–272. doi:10.1207/S15327884MCA0704_02

Wertsch, J. V. (1981). The Concept of activity in soviet psychology. An introduction. In J. V. Wertsch (Ed.), *The concept of activity in soviet psychology* (pp. 3–36). Armonk: M.E. Sharpe, Inc.

Wertsch, J. V. (1991). *Voices of the mind. A sociocultural approach to mediated action.* Cambridge, MA: Harvard University Press.

Wertsch, J. V. (1998). *Mind as action.* New York, NY: Oxford University Press.

Widén, P. (2015). Kvalitativ textanalys [Qualitative text analysis]. In A. Fejes & R. Thornberg (Eds.), *Handbok i kvalitativ analys* [Handbook of qualitative analysis] (pp. 176–193). Stockholm: Liber AB.

Virkkunen, J., & Newnham, D. S. (2013). *The change laboratory. A tool for collaborative development of work and education.* Rotterdam, The Netherlands: Sense Publishers.

Wittrock, M. C. (Ed.). (1986). *Handbook of research on teaching.* New York, NY: MacMillan Publishing Company.

REFERENCES

Wolcott, H. F. (1994). The elementary school principal: Notes from a field study. In H. F. Wolcott (Ed.), *Transforming qualitative data: Description, analysis, and interpretation* (pp. 115–148). Thousand Oaks, CA: Sage Publications, Inc.

Wolcott, H. (2001). *Writing up qualitative research* (2nd ed.). Thousand Oaks, CA: Sage Publications, Inc.

Wolcott, H. (2008). *Ethnography – A way of seeing* (2nd ed.). Lanham, MD: AltaMira Press.

Wolf, M. A. (1992). *A thrice-told tale: Feminism, postmordernism, and ethnographic responsibility.* Palo Alto, CA: Stanford University Press.

Yin, R. K. (2009). *Case study research. Design and methods* (4th ed.). Thousand Oaks, CA: Sage Publications, Inc.

Zimmerman, B. J. (2006). Development and adaption of expertise: The role of self-regulatory processes and beliefs. In K. A. Ericsson, N. Charness, P. J. Feltovich, & R. R. Hoffman (Eds.), *The Cambridge handbook of expertise and expert performance* (pp. 705–722). Cambridge: Cambridge University Press.

Index

abductive approach 32
abstract objectivism 9, 10
acting subject 15, 16
action learning 3, 74
action learning circle 18, 19, 127
action-oriented knowledge 12
activity system 6, 13–16, 18–22, 24, 89, 104, 109, 127
analytical categories 114, 115, 129
analytical unit 13, 14, 109
anonymity 118
appropriate sample 37, 51, 125
asking questions 7, 45, 57, 74, 77, 78, 99–100, 108, 132
assumption 32, 36–38, 59, 60, 69, 80, 81, 88, 111, 119, 128
auto-ethnography 63
axial coding 90, 91, 93, 95
axiology 6, 34, 36

bedrock 57, 126, 128
behaviourism 8
bracket 59
bricolage 33
bricoleur 33

case studies
    collective case study 52
    instrumental case study 52
    internal case study 47, 52
    single case 52
clarification question 77
cognitive theory 9
cognitivism 8, 10
collaborative action research 28
collective activity 14, 15
community 15, 17, 20, 35, 46, 71, 109
comprehensive theories 8, 29, 97, 98, 122
confidence 40, 43, 45, 118
consent 47, 127, 135–136
consent form 47, 118, 136
constant comparisons 7, 51, 59, 66, 86–96, 99, 103–109, 116, 129, 131
constructivism 8, 10, 11
constructivist theory 8, 11

context 2, 6, 9, 10, 12, 13, 15, 19, 21, 24, 30, 33–35, 38, 41, 42, 44, 45, 52, 53, 56, 57, 59, 60–64, 67–70, 72, 77, 79, 83, 89, 93–96, 98, 102, 110–112, 115, 117, 119, 121, 123, 126–128, 133
contextual information 69, 83, 127
contextual knowledge 112
contingency matrix 98
continuous analyses 18, 40
contradiction
    primary 16
    secondary 16
    tertiary 16, 21
    quaternary 16, 21
conversation analysis 7, 20, 22, 51, 66–67, 86, 125
core category 91, 95–97, 102
credibility 111, 113, 115, 116
cultural portrait 55, 56

data analyses
    analysis of documents 65
    categorical aggregation 54
    chronological analytical method 65
    constant comparative analysis method 86–96, 103
    conversation analysis 66–67
    cultural analysesm 57
    D-analysis 103–109
    dialogic/performative analysis 65
    direct analysis 53–54
    Stevick-Colaizzi-Keen method 61
    structural analysis 65
    text analysis 65–66
    thematic analysis 62, 65
    three-dimensional analytical approach 65
    visual analysis 65
data collection
    audio recording 82, 83
    development interview 79
    focus-group interview 78–79
    follow-up interview 74, 78, 83
    intervening focus-group interview 79–80
    observation 68–69

INDEX

observation book   80
participatory observation   69–71
semi-structured interview   73
structured interview   72
unstructured interview   72–73
video recording   82, 83
deductive approach   32
dependability   111
descriptive analysis   59, 85, 102, 129
descriptive categories   128
descriptive psychological
    phenomenology   58
descriptive text   37, 40, 55, 125
development process   1, 3, 5, 12, 13, 16, 19–24, 30, 40, 42, 43, 46, 50, 94, 97, 98, 100, 101, 112, 116. 117, 123, 127
development question   2, 3, 17, 18, 19, 22, 23, 30, 38–39, 43, 49, 76, 98, 103, 116
development tool   50, 117
development work research (DWR)   1, 2, 5, 6, 12, 16, 24, 29, 30, 37–39, 41–47, 49–51, 72, 79, 86, 87, 98, 103–105, 109, 111, 112, 114–118, 121, 127, 128, 130
developmental transfer   21
diagrams   96–97
dialogic intersubjectivity   110
dimensions   66, 94, 96, 97, 99–101, 114
division of labour   15, 20

elementary actions   13
emic perspective   27, 32–33, 35, 56
empirical approach   8
enlightenment   26
epistemological   8, 51, 68
epistemology   6, 34–36
epoché   59
etic perspective   27, 33, 35, 57, 69
ethical principles   7, 35, 41, 110, 115, 117–119, 128
ethnographic studies   7, 20–22, 27, 36, 42, 51, 55–58, 69, 73, 76, 77, 80, 86, 118, 126
expansive learning cycle   12, 16, 17, 19, 22–24, 45, 126
expressionism   28
externalization   12

far-out comparisons   100–101
first-order description   61
first-person perspective   121
fish in the water   56

flip-flop strategy   101
formative intervention   12
formative interventionist researcher   12

Geisteswissenschaften   26
general theory   96
goal-directed actions   11, 15, 22, 94, 98
going native   56
grounded theory   86, 87, 119

hermeneutic phenomenology   58, 60, 62
heterogeneous group   60

idealism   8
IGP method   3
impressionist   31
individual action   15
inductive approach   32
informed consent   118, 132
innovative circle   18
intermediary aid   15
intermediate theories   29, 37
inter-mental level   12
internalization   12
interpretation   32–34, 54, 57–59, 65, 80, 86, 87, 89–91, 96, 114–116, 128, 129
intersubjective   60, 69, 110–111
intersubjectivity   110
intra-mental level   12
in-vivo codes   102

knowledge-based development   30

lesson study   3, 74
life phase   63, 65
lifeworld   34, 59
logbook   35, 44, 70, 80, 86, 90, 111, 128

main categories   91, 94, 95, 97, 103, 129, 131
main research question   37–39, 73, 76, 112, 113, 123–125, 131, 133
making comparisons
master's thesis   7, 29, 35, 50, 121, 126, 131, 133–134
mediating artefact   11–13, 15, 20, 21, 103, 109
member checking   97, 113–115
memos   96–97, 116
meta-cognitive attitude   22
meta-cognitive competence   22
meta-learning   23

meta-text   124
meta-view   46, 111
micro-ethnographic study   20–22, 76, 77, 80, 86, 118
mind   3, 8, 10, 27, 31, 48, 56, 71, 85, 112, 115, 128
mirror data   12, 43, 46
methodological   8, 36, 37, 77–78
methodology   6, 12, 20, 34–36, 51, 52, 86, 133
model questions   76
moderator   78

narrative study   7, 20, 42, 51, 62–65, 73, 77, 86
naturalistic   33, 68
naturalistic generalization   34, 54, 116
natural setting   32–33, 37, 68
Naturwissenschaften   26
neutral   36, 64, 72, 80, 111
neutral object   13

object   11, 15–18, 20, 21, 43, 59, 98, 103, 104, 109
object is the true motive   21, 43
objectivity   69, 111
objectivity principle   56, 69, 111
observer roles
    active membership role   70, 71
    active participant role   71
    balanced participant role   70
    complete observer   69, 70
    complete membership role   70, 71
    complete participant   69–71
    observer-as-participant   69, 70, 82
    participant-as-observer   69, 70
    passive participant role   70
    peripheral membership role   70, 71
    peripheral participant role   70
ontology   6, 34, 36
ontological   8, 34
open coding   90, 91, 93
open coding phase   91, 93, 95

paradigm   8–10, 29, 34, 37, 51, 57, 69, 93–95, 114
participants' perspective   32, 73, 131
participatory action research   28
phenomenological study   77, 109, 125
phonemic   33
phonetic   33
positivism   8, 10

primary circle   23, 46
probing questions   73–77, 83
properties   20, 21, 34, 94, 96, 97, 99–101
proximity   35, 44, 67
pseudonyms   118
psychoanalytic theory   9
psychological phenomenology   58–60
psychological stimulation   9
psycho-analytical perspective   27

qualitative method   1, 6, 25–40, 51–67, 86, 127
quotations   7, 56, 82, 120, 121, 131, 132

R&D model   6, 22, 23, 46, 127
rationalism   8
realism   8
reflection   4, 9, 18, 20, 21, 23, 24, 50, 80, 101, 106, 108, 109, 130, 132
reflexive   110
reflexive process   29, 110
reflexivity   122
reliability   111–115, 119
replicate   112
research instrument   30
research questions   5, 20–22, 24, 29, 30, 37–39, 46, 48, 49, 53, 55, 59, 66, 68, 71, 73, 74, 76, 80, 88, 102, 110, 112, 113, 116, 120, 123–125, 131, 133
research report   78, 110
researcher's eye   24, 29
researcher's gaze   29
researcher role
    distance   44
    insider   33, 44, 70
    on the sidelines   42, 47–49, 72
    outsider   33, 35, 44, 70
    proximity   44
    the interacting researcher   42–45
researcher's plateau   24
response
response categories   72
retro-spective description   60
rules   15, 21, 26, 27, 53, 109

secondary circle   23, 24, 46, 127
second-order description   60, 61
selective coding   90, 96
selective coding phase   91, 95, 96,
self-regulated   22

INDEX

sensitising concepts   89
socio-cultural theory   10–12, 15, 89, 129
stimulus   13, 14
sub-categories   91, 93–95, 97, 102–104, 131
subjective individualism   9
subjectivity   29, 32, 37, 38, 56, 59, 69, 80, 83, 110–112, 121, 122, 128
substantive theories   29, 30, 37, 96, 116, 122, 129
sub-question   37–39, 73, 112, 123, 124, 131, 133
surveys   72–80

tabula rasa   8
teacher researcher   70
tension   6, 15, 16, 19–21, 26, 59, 63, 109, 127
text analysis   7, 51, 65–66, 86
theoretical analysis   102, 129
theoretical comparisons   100
theoretical models   10, 29, 37, 52, 122, 126
theoretical sensitivity   87, 88
the other   25, 27, 28
thick descriptions   25, 33, 34, 54, 56, 90, 116, 126, 128
thin descriptions   7, 34, 121, 126

thinking tool   33, 34, 110, 117, 125
timetable   4, 109
traditional qualitative methodologies   1, 25–40
traditional qualitative research   1, 13, 25, 28, 29, 32, 34–37, 39, 68, 69
transcribe   77, 83
transcription   61, 64, 65, 91
transferability   111, 113, 116
triangulation   113, 114
trustworthiness   112, 113

unit of analysis   15, 19, 89
units of meaning   61
universal knowledge   110

validation   97
validity
    internal validity   111
    external validity   111

wave the red flag   101, 102
world   8–11, 26, 28, 29, 32, 36, 66, 67, 71, 87

zone of proximal development   17, 29, 60, 89